CHINA DAY BY DAY

CHINA
DAY BY DAY

EILEEN HSÜ-BALZER

RICHARD J. BALZER

FRANCIS L. K. HSU

NEW HAVEN AND LONDON, YALE UNIVERSITY PRESS, 1974

Published with assistance from the foundation
established in memory of James Wesley Cooper
of the Class of 1865, Yale College.

Designed by Sally Sullivan
and set in Times Roman type.
Printed in the United States of America by
Eastern Press, Inc., New Haven, Connecticut.

Published in Great Britain, Europe, and Africa by
Yale University Press, Ltd., London. Distributed in
Latin America by Kaiman & Polon, Inc., New York
City; in Australasia and Southeast Asia by John Wiley &
Sons Australasia Pty. Ltd., Sydney; in India by UBS
Publishers' Distributors Pvt., Ltd., Delhi; in Japan by
John Weatherhill, Inc., Tokyo.

to our Grandmother, Chia Chia

CONTENTS

ACKNOWLEDGMENTS

Many people helped us create this book. We would like to mention with particular gratitude Bob and Joanne Balzer, Jane Isay and Sally Sullivan of the Yale University Press, Sven Martsen, John Hill, and Vera Hsu and Penny Hsu, all of whose encouragement, talents, and efforts are reflected in this book.

We would also like to express our appreciation to the honorable Wang Kuo-chuan, former chairman of the Chinese Foreign Friendship Association, and to the many Chinese guides and interpreters, official and unofficial, who made this trip so rewarding, both intellectually and personally.

Eileen Hsü-Balzer
Richard Balzer
Francis L. K. Hsu

INTRODUCTION: HOW TO UNDERSTAND CHINA

Few Americans know about the hermit kingdom of Bhutan. But who does not know about China? In fact, most Americans not only know about China but also hold varied and conflicting opinions about her.

This diversity of views has increased considerably since the Communist Revolution of 1949 and is likely to increase further as more Americans of unlike backgrounds return from visits to China. There are those who are irreconcilably opposed to Communism wherever it occurs, in contrast to others who are greatly impressed by the economic and political achievements of the new regime. Some complain the Chinese have no freedom, while others see the present regimentation as temporary and assume capitalist trends will follow economic development as inevitably in the People's Republic as they seem to have in the U.S.S.R.

Are we doomed to the conclusion that such diverse attitudes can never be reconciled? Or is there a possibility that we can arrive at some reasonably clear understanding of China which all intelligent men and women can more or less accept?

I submit the latter eventuality is not beyond our grasp and that the easiest way to achieve this understanding is to compare the way in which the Chinese versus the American individual feels about himself and relates to his fellow men as well as to the rest of the world. When we have done this, I believe we shall have a set of keys whereby we may understand not only the Chinese way of life but also why Communism has triumphed in China, what it is the Communists are trying to do, and how successful they are in attaining their goals.

All human beings must live in association with other human beings. Even David Henry Thoreau did not really have his heart set on solitude. If he had, why would he have written so many journals? What Thoreau wanted was not real solitude but a club of solitude lovers. Human beings all wish to find a place among fellow human beings, to maintain it, and to improve it. Consequently, the problem of understanding China in contrast to the United States is one of understanding their respective ways of dealing with interpersonal relations.

Four basic attributes characterize the Chinese in their personal relations. The first is *continuity*. Continuity describes the situation whereby, once a personal link of any sort has been established between two individuals, it tends to last a long time. The obverse of this is *discontinuity*, characterized by a brittleness in interpersonal links. Of course these terms are absolutes, which rarely, if ever, govern human affairs. But their contrast is still unambiguous when viewed in relative terms. A relationship lasting five years is more continuous than one lasting two; and one that lasts a lifetime is more continuous than one lasting ten years, and so on.

Take the parent-child relationship, for instance. In the Chinese scheme of things, the link lasts forever. A man remains a son of his parents, regardless of age, and the matter goes both ways. While the son retains much of his attitude of respect and subordination toward his parents, they continue their command and succor of him throughout life. Of course as the sons grow older and become more able, as the parents age and become less active, there will be inevitable changes. But such changes only strengthen the link. For the Chinese say: "The first thirty years of a man's life, respect the son for his father; the second thirty years of a man's life, respect the father for his son." Thus the link continues.

And this continuity radiates into every other kind of relationship, in or outside the kinship sphere. Friendship among the Chinese tends to last a long time, in contrast to that among Americans which tends to be short-lived. The Chinese look askance at persons who keep changing friends. In fact, a common Chinese reason for seeking out a friend is that "he is such an old friend, I've got to see him," but a common American justification for discarding a friend is that "we have nothing in common any more." In the former case, the oldness of the link is reason enough for its continuation, while, in the latter case, it is of no significance.

This provides an important key to understanding other Chinese customs. Chinese have always preferred sons to daughters. They needed sons to continue their male family lines. They even used that requirement as one of the main reasons for concubinage. Not only did they prefer sons, they also wanted all their sons to be married. Since the sons did not have to wait till they were financially independent to enter matrimony, they could marry young, they could take wives in the name of securing daughters-in-law for their parents. Under the circumstances, arranged marriages were natural, and ancestor worship was a logical consequence.

The second attribute of Chinese relations is *inclusiveness,* in contrast to American *exclusiveness*. Exclusiveness, as expressed by the notion of individual privacy, which Americans value so highly, has never been a point of Chinese contention. Inclusiveness means that whatever is parents' business is the business of their children, and vice versa. And, as an extension, neighbors, friends, colleagues, teachers and students, employers and employees share in each other's lives to an extent impossible for Americans.

Chinese couples think nothing of asking a third party, such as an aunt, a parent, a neighbor, or a friend to adjudicate their quarrels. Many Chinese offer to arbitrate quarrels of any kind, and they are admired and respected by the community for settling disputes and pacifying angers.

There are other patterns of behavior indicative of Chinese inclusiveness. For example, the Chinese, as a matter of course, would consult several doctors, either serially or simultaneously. Several doctors of differing qualities and approaches might answer the house call of a single desperate but well-to-do patient. In fact, while being treated by doctors, the Chinese patient and his family thought nothing of consulting oracles or taking the advice of a knowledgeable monk. This used to upset Western doctors in the 30s who were on the staff of the Peking Union Medical College (now National Capital Hospital, after being named Anti-Imperialist Hospital during the Great Cultural Revolution).

Inclusiveness is further evident in the Chinese attitude toward religion. The Western approach to religion is well known. It exemplifies exclusiveness par excellence. One is not only a Christian, but a Protestant or Catholic; not only a Protestant but Methodist or Baptist; not only Methodist or Baptist but a member of the First Methodist Church of Evanston or of the Hemenway Methodist Church of Evanston. The Chinese, on the other hand, belonged to no temple. They had no idea of congregation. They went to a particular temple in accordance with the needs of the occasion, and they even shopped from god to god until they found one who would satisfy their needs. For special emergencies, such as cholera epidemics, rituals would be performed to all known gods, including Christ and Mohammed, even though the worshipers were not Christians or Moslems. That is inclusiveness.

Authority is the third Chinese attribute, and its opposite is the American attribute of *volition,* of which the concept of freedom is its most essential expression. The Chinese have never developed the concept of freedom and have never fought any wars in the name of freedom. Authority means that commands must be given and obeyed, that it is perfectly in accordance with the order of things for the people to be divided into the governors and the governed. The former should be wise and experienced, and able to guide the less wise and less experienced. The latter, in their turn, should guide those inferior to them.

Consequently, Chinese parents do not have to play the friendship game with their children. Growing up does not imply the change of a vertical relationship with the parents into a horizontal one, as American educators, under the influence of the attribute of volition, would theorize. Since Chinese parents maintain their position of superiority, as parents, maturity in the Chinese scheme of things has always meant the acquisition of the wisdom and the experience to know how to act as sons with reference to parents and how to act as parents with reference to sons. Given such a premise, subordination to and exercise of authority in the Chinese context differs vastly from the American approach to authority. A Chinese superior, be he father, boss, or political leader, can exercise his authority without having to pretend that it comes from a higher authority—as his American counterpart tends to do. Likewise, a Chinese subordinate, be he son, employee, or political follower, suffers less from the fear of being humiliated that might plague his American counterpart. In the celebrated classical Chinese novel *The Dream of the Red Chamber* the following episode occurred. The hero of the book, Chia Pao-yu, was being publicly whipped by his father, Chia Cheng, for sexual malfeasance which led to the suicide of a young maid. The father, a high government official and head of his large household, was extremely angry and made a spectacle of the son's punishment. Some servant devoted to the young master secretly informed his widowed paternal grandmother of the goings-on, since it was known she was highly indulgent of the young man. She stormed to the scene.

"Let him kill me first and then the boy; that will at least be a clean sweep!" she screamed. Seeing the old lady's rage, Chia Cheng fell on his knees before his mother and humbly explained to her that he merely punished his son as a duty to his glorious ancestors. Refusing to be pacified, the old lady wept as she uttered more angry words and loudly ordered her retinue to prepare for her departure from home with *her* daughter-in-law and *her* grandson.

Like their American sisters, some Chinese women in the olden days resorted to the tactic of going home to mother as a way of hitting back at their men. In this case, however, the old lady used the tactic against her son, not her husband. And since she probably had no mother to go to, she simply said she was going to the southern capital.

In desperation, Chia Cheng, acknowledging his guilt, hit his forehead on the ground repeatedly but the act had no effect on his mother. There ensued a most noisy spectacle of maids carrying the severely beaten son on a stretcher to his grandmother's quarters, Chia Cheng's wife loudly lamenting her son's unfortunate fate, the grandmother sobbing uncontrollably, and the crestfallen high official bringing up the rear trying once more to talk his mother into forgiveness.

Of course the author of the novel dressed up the episode for dramatic effect, but it was an episode well understood by Chinese and not uncommon among them. Did the autocratic high official, so severe with his own son but so docile in front of his own mother, lose any social esteem before the assembled family and servants and relatives? Not at all. A Chinese man who obeyed his own widowed mother so publicly would gain in esteem. Such behavior would likely be an important influence in support of a man's greatness by his posthumous biographers, in the same way that an American would be praised posthumously for some exceptional act of valor in war.

The three attributes just analyzed support each other. Inclusiveness is another form of continuity; it is continuity in space as opposed to continuity in time. When I keep my friends for a lifetime my behavior exemplifies continuity. But when my friends' relatives also become my friends by virtue of our friendship in the first place, that is a case of inclusiveness. When I want to advance myself to follow in the footsteps of my father and his forebears, that represents not only continuity in time but also inclusiveness, because more individuals than myself have determined my decision in the selection of a career.

Likewise, the attribute of authority works well with inclusiveness and continuity. It makes it logical for me to follow in the footsteps of my forebears, because I am not prompted by the desire to make all the decisions for myself. I can afford to let other individuals affect or even determine my choices, because such a pattern of decision-making increases my social esteem as an adult.

Inclusiveness, continuity, and authority, in conjunction with each other, thus gave Chinese culture some of its peculiar characteristics. The Chinese were less afraid than their American counterparts to grow old. They could afford to roll with the punches because old age increased rather than decreased their social importance among later generations. The American fear of old age, and the strenuous defenses against it, as when grandmothers wear miniskirts, stems from a realization that the elderly simply have no place in the existing scheme of things. With a pattern of interpersonal relationships founded on exclusiveness, discontinuity, and volition the situation cannot be otherwise. Marriage necessarily involves a deep break in the psychological intimacy with one's parents, and maturity necessarily means doing what one wants to do, not what one's parents decree. The young must therefore bear the responsibility of independently seeking a mate, finding a career, and, most important, achieving an identity. But these and other problems can all be overcome and many self-reliant men, steeped in the notion of conquest, can usually find the courage and the means to do it. However, for the aging and aged, there is nothing left. Death conquers everyone with equal finality, but the conditions under which the last phases of life are so discontinuous from earlier stages make aging so unpalatable.* The problem is one of whether or not failing physical powers are compensated for by increased authority and prestige.

Continuity, inclusiveness, and authority are commensurate with maintenance of the status quo and stagnation. These attributes do not generate intrasocietal impetuses to change. A culture of this type is guided more by the old than the young, encourages its people to adhere to tradition rather than seek improvements, and fosters a guiding

philosophy of contentment rather than of change and progress. It is now generally acknowledged among scholars that China has the world's longest continuous civilization, but the same scholars have yet to appreciate the fact that this historical longevity was at least in part founded on the fact that the Chinese population was centripetal as contrasted to its centrifugal European counterpart.

When we consider the development from ancient times of the civilizations of Europe (e.g. Greece and Rome) and the Near East (e.g. Israel and Assyria), we find that, in contrast to China, there occurred in different localities, a series of rises and falls, which in most cases precipitated the loss of a traditional way of life. A segment of the old population would move to a new home, losing little time in making their claim to having founded something totally new. This pattern was also, very obviously, repeated in the development of New World cultures including that of the United States. It was this kind of pattern that enabled Arnold Toynbee to characterize many civilizations as having died.

On the other hand, the Chinese, like these other cultures, began, at around 2,000 B.C. (the Bronze Age in Europe), with a small population that was, in fact, a heterogeneous one, speaking many tongues and practicing many customs. This heterogeneity was still visible some 1,500 years later, at the time of Confucius. But, as the Chinese population grew in size, the Chinese society never left the middle Yellow River basin where the distinctive character of the Chinese civilization began.

The present-day world distribution of Chinese and European populations bears eloquent testimony to these different processes. Today, Europe, outside European Russia, has a population of 450,000,000. But, the white population of the two Americas alone comes to 500,000,000. On the other hand, while China's population today is somewhere around 750,000,000, the so-called "overseas chinese," including those in all South Seas countries, number no more than 15,000,000 to 19,000,000. In short, there are more Europeans outside

---

*Apparently not every phase of American life equally exemplifies discontinuity. I am interested to note that in the relationship test for members of the family the booklet, *Your Federal Income Tax* (1973) states: "Once any of the above relationships have been established by marriage, they will not be terminated by divorce" (p. 5).

of their historical base than in it, while less than 3 percent of the Chinese are far from their traditional homeland.

Lest any reader think this was because the Chinese lacked navigational or other technical skills, it should be pointed out that some sixty years before Columbus started his voyage to the New World with three relatively small boats and about a hundred people, a Chinese fleet manned by some 20,000 people, under the command of Admiral Cheng, conquered all the way from China to the East African coast. Admiral Cheng made seven such expeditions but the common Chinese people did not follow his conquests.

We come now to the fourth attribute governing Chinese relationships, and that is *asexuality* contrasting sharply with Western *sexuality*. Besides being the core of the family, making biological continuation of the group possible, sex exists as the strongest bond between males and females. However, as with food, we can indulge in sex with moderation or excess. We will consume food whether we have pornography of food just as we will enjoy sex whether or not we make a fetish of sex.

The Chinese assign sexuality to its proper place and do not allow it to appear elsewhere. Their attitude is not a reflection of Puritanism, which says that sex is evil and therefore must not be enjoyed under any circumstances. Rather, the Chinese believe that sex is bad only when practiced with the wrong partner (such as someone else's wife), in the wrong place (such as in a public park), and at the wrong time (such as during broad daylight). Otherwise it was perfectly natural and certainly to be enjoyed. Sexuality was also evident in prostitution and in some popular dramas. In all other contexts, sex was either completely absent or entirely subordinate to considerations of social acceptability.

For example, most Chinese novels do not concern themselves with male-female relationships. Such relationships may appear as brief interludes having little or nothing to do with the actual plot. In Chinese novels that do concern themselves with romance, the plot may begin with two lovers who meet and consummate their relationship outside of wedlock. The rest of the book would concentrate on how to legitimize the liaison. The same attitude is evident in the fine arts. Chinese paintings, through the centuries, featured landscapes, still lifes, and animals, including fish and insects; there was little emphasis on the human subject, and females were rarely depicted. Except for expressly pornographic art, Chinese painters never were concerned with the naked beauty of the female form. Human figures were always portrayed as minute in relation to the landscape, bridges, and houses, or they were fully clothed to represent their social status or activity.

Not only does this sharply contrast with Western art and literature, but the contrast also corresponds to actual life styles. A brief look at Western advertisements will leave no doubt as to the overwhelming role sex plays, whether the goods advertised are cigarettes, mouthwashes, deodorants, travel, drinks, clothes, or even homes. A cigar manufacturer promotes his product by having a girl with white feathers on her head wink at the viewers and say: "You get a lot more than smoke." A few months ago, the *Wall Street Journal* reported that a California real-estate developer was describing his new homes as having, "three rooms, two baths, and wall-to-wall sex." Sex appeal is even an ingredient in American politics, which is why movie actors and actresses are so visible during election campaigns. There has been nothing comparable in Chinese affairs, before or after the coming of the West.

Religion is another area where Chinese and Western attitudes toward sex diverge. For example, the most popular Western religion is Christianity, which centers on the myth of the Virgin Birth. Some readers may ask, since the myth of the Virgin Birth denies the facts of life, does it not indicate asexuality? My reply is that the myth of the Virgin Birth especially signifies sexuality for it reminds me of an old Chinese story. A peasant came into a windfall of 300 silver pieces. After burying them in a pit in his backyard for safekeeping, he was still fearful someone might mistakenly stumble onto his treasure, so he put a sign over it saying: "There are no 300 pieces of silver here."

The Chinese knew several versions of the Virgin Birth, but they made little or no use of it. Many American readers today know something about *Tao Te Ching* the book of Lao Tze, the alleged founder of Taoism. But how many have heard that, besides having been carried by his mother for eighty years so that he was born very old with beard and wrinkles, Lao Tze was born of a virgin? Few Chinese and probably not a single American have ever heard that the Ching (Manchu) dynasty was supposed to have originated from a virgin. Three sisters were taking a dip in a secluded stream. As they frolicked in water, a bird landed on the bank, chirped loudly, dropped something, and flew away. The youngest of the sisters, a mere child, went to investigate and found a beautiful tiny egg. She put it in her mouth and swallowed it involuntarily. She became pregnant, and the son she bore was Nurhachu, the founder of the dynasty. The birth myths associated with Lao Tze and Nurhachu are so obscure because the Chinese lent them no importance.

As I already indicated, the Chinese approach to sexuality is to assign it to restricted areas. Consequently, the good family women in China learned to conduct themselves with great decorum; in fact, they rarely appeared in public. They did meet men other than their parents, brothers, and husbands, but when they were introduced to their husbands' male friends, they would never exhibit familiarity, let alone coquettishness. In fact, a male guest could compliment his hostess on her cooking, on how well she brought up her children, or how efficiently she ran her house, but never on the charm of her dress or her beauty. The latter would be a breach of good etiquette and a cause for serious offense. That is why, even after the fall of the imperial dynasty, social dancing never found much acceptance in China.

It may be seen that asexuality functions well with the other three Chinese attributes; continuity, inclusiveness, and authority just as sexuality is in accord with three Western attributes of discontinuity, exclu-

siveness, and volition.* In this latter case, sex is exclusive, typically subject to ups and downs, and it fades away altogether with old age. It is certainly dependent upon the voluntary cooperation of both partners. When, on the other hand, sexuality is confined to its proper but limited domain, it supports the attributes of continuity, inclusiveness, and authority. For example, sons cannot fulfill their duties and obligations to their parents, and please them, by insisting on love at first sight and freedom in the choice of mates. Their relationship with their parents will necessarily suffer if, after marriage, sons only cleave to their wives. And, while authority is generally incompatible with sexuality (husbands usually have trouble teaching wives to drive and analysts cannot help their mistresses overcome neuroses), a leadership based on authority can be far more long lasting (continuous) than one based on sex appeal.

These distinctions are confirmed in the respective ways the Chinese and the Westerners have dealt with the myth of the Primeval Flood. Myths are not historical reality. They do not tell us what actually happened. But they do tell us a great deal about the psychic pressures and expectations of the people who shaped them and gave them currency over long periods of time.

The Western reader is generally familiar with the sequence of events after Noah became the chosen man and was informed by God of the impending disaster. He packed up his wife, three sons, and their wives, as well as a pair of every kind of animal in a ship to escape it. When the flood subsided, the ship landed on Ararat. After thanking the Lord, by appropriate rituals, Noah and his wife apparently lived for a while together with his sons and their wives. Then, Noah drank the wine he had made, and under its influence, masturbated in his tent. Ham, seeing his father exposed, told his two brothers about it; the sons were all dis-

---

*The dominant attributes within other kinship systems do not necessarily fit each other so well. The conflict of within-system attributes creates other problems that we cannot deal with here [see Francis L. K. Hsu, *Kinship and Culture* (Chicago: Aldine Publishing Co., 1971), pp. 3–30].

gusted with Noah. There ensued some kind of quarrel, and Noah then blessed Shem and Japheth, cursed Ham, and condemned Ham's son Canaan and his descendants to eternal slavery. All the sons and their wives then dispersed to different parts of the earth.

According to the Chinese version, emperors Yao and Shun (said to have reigned, respectively, from 2358–2258 B.C. and 2258–2206 B.C.) were great and moral rulers. In Yao's old age a terrible flood devastated the country. Yao appointed an official to control the flood, but the official was unsuccessful. Yao then appointed the able and popular man Shun as his successor to the throne, who proceeded to execute the unsuccessful official and appoint the criminal's son Yu in his place. Yu worked for many years, going all over the country, and finally succeeded in controlling the flood. During his many years of duty, he passed by his own house three different times (during his first year of absence, his wife gave birth to a son), but he was so mindful of his duty that he did not enter it even once. After his success, Yu was appointed the next emperor by a grateful Shun. Hence, Yu not only accomplished what his father failed, but also brought honor to his elder.

Thus, in the Western version the myth focuses on the individual and his spouse (exclusiveness and sexuality), disregard for the aged, since Noah's parents were not in the picture at all (discontinuity), a chosen man and his immediate family moving away from the homeland and from traditional authority (discontinuity and volition), dispersion into different parts of the world, never to return to their point of origin (discontinuity). The Chinese version, however, emphasizes the group and tradition (inclusiveness and authority), staying in the same area (continuity and inclusiveness) with no notion of the chosen man (inclusiveness), with individuals working on the flood at the command of their superiors (authority), and with the son completing the work the father failed (continuity). The Chinese hero's duties to the larger group even overshadowed his conjugal relationship with his wife (asexuality).

It is upon these fundamental concepts governing Chinese relationships that the new Chinese government must build a new state, a new society, and, as it often publicly proclaims, a new man. What are the objectives of the new government? How much of the old does it wish to replace? And finally, how far has it changed the traditional patterns of Chinese interpersonal relationships?

To begin with, it was the West that insisted on discovering China and not vice versa. Once discovered, China was still happy to carry on as she had for thousands of years, but the West would not leave China alone, and the Chinese system, though coherent in its own way, was unequal to the power of the intruders. Having been accustomed to follow in the footsteps of their ancestors (continuity and authority) nineteenth century Chinese were still using bows and arrows and junks with sails when their adversaries were equipped with firearms and gunboats propelled by steam. There was no doubt as to the outcome in such an encounter.

Another area of Chinese inferiority was that of human organization. Since the parent-child configuration was the primary human network, inclusiveness and continuity meant that the Chinese did not leave the kinship group. As time went on, the average individual was enmeshed in a sizable kinship network, its size limited only by birth, death, and marriage. For this reason, the tendency for a person to stay within this network outweighed his tendency to move away. Furthermore, should he go elsewhere, he would want to maintain the kinship ties and later to return to it. Ancestor worship, detailed genealogical records, clan graveyards, arranged marriages, the ethics of filial piety, marriage by all, preference for sons, inequality of parents and sons before the law, low divorce rate, high nepotism, these were among the characteristic features of the culture complex.

As a result, no secondary groups of any moment developed to serve as an effective organizational link between the kinship setting and the national setting. Industries and commerce were family businesses. No public companies existed with objective and impersonal criteria for hiring, promotion, and dismissal. Even the armed forces were run in a personal way. They varied greatly in quality depending upon commanders, because the officers and men were attached to their commanders. The government bureaucracy was founded on an age-old accumulation of customs and usages, with each new head bringing his own relatives, friends and former subordinates as a matter of course. The only sizable secondary organizations were some of the secret societies made up of hustlers and outlaws, and even they cohered in the kinship model. The bureaucrats in government operated as powerful men from their own separate clans and localities.

Dr. Sun Yat-sen, the man who led the 1911 revolution that toppled the Manchu dynasty, characterized the Chinese as "a tray of loose sands." Strictly speaking he was not really correct. The Chinese did indeed cohere, but the center of their solidarity was the kinship and locality. Chinese society was a collection of these relatively small groups without any means for larger collective action toward achieving objectives not decreed by the past. It was no accident that in much of his revolutionary effort even Dr. Sun had to make use of the secret societies, just as Americans employed local mafiosi as intelligence agents and underground organizers against the Nazi and Fascist forces during World War II.

As a result of these deficiencies, China was first reduced by Western powers to a semicolonial status and then threatened with dismemberment. The Chinese reacted with a series of uprisings, rebellions, and revolutions; the more notable ones were the Taiping Rebellion (1850–65), the Boxer Uprising (1900), and the Republican Revolution (1911–12) which finally made China a republic, at least nominally.

But the overthrow of the Imperial dynasty only ushered in the era of the warlords. It was not until 1928 that the Nationalists, under Chiang Kai-shek, more or less brought most of China into a sort of political and economic unity. By then, however, Japan, not satisfied with occupation of

Manchuria in 1931, embarked on a course of total conquest which eventually led to Pearl Harbor, to the 1945 surrender of Japan that marked the end of World War II, and, finally in 1949, to the ascension of Communist rule in China.

I briefly recite these events solely for the purpose of indicating that the Communist Revolution of 1949 was neither an isolated nor sudden event; instead, it was the last of a series of Chinese responses to foreign encroachment, which not only prevented the Chinese from continuing their traditional way of life but also exacerbated China's own internal problems and threatened her with total subjugation.

The objectives of the new Chinese government share, therefore, a great deal in common with those sought after by most of its modern predecessors. Briefly, there are only two objectives: the first is to enable China to establish a position in the modern world commensurate with her esteemed status in the pre-modern world, for a population that has known greatness and still has intimate psychological links with that greatness cannot long endure inferiority .The second objective is to restore China's greatness through industrialization in Western terms and to accomplish this with some rapidity. Here, China has no alternative, since the rules have already been dictated by industrial-based powers.

Judging by results, the new Chinese government is already well on the way to achieving her first objective. She certainly has stood up to the modern world. There are no more foreign troops on her soil or foreign warships in her waters. She is treated as an equal in the capitals of all the nations that recognize her (and there are mighty few which don't). Furthermore, whatever happens or is said in China makes world headlines. In fact, China, today, is in many respects admired and even emulated by many peoples, especially those of the Third World. Throughout our travels in and outside of China, we found no Chinese, whether favorably or unfavorably inclined toward the Communist regime, who did not take pride in China's rising world status. The fact that she is not asking for, but giving foreign aid, adds greatly to this pride.

Industrially, China has a long way to go. The Chinese government functionaries, party cadres, and ordinary workers, alike, told us China is still a poor country by comparison with the United States and other developed nations. But the Chinese make no secret of their determination to industrialize and to industrialize with speed. Today it is agreed that the Great Leap Forward movement was not an economic success. In fact, many agree that it led to setbacks that contributed to the three years of crop failure (1959–61). But the Leap was an expression of China's impatience to catch up with the industrially advanced nations of the world.

Again, judging by results and comparing conditions today with those in the 30s and the 40s, and with those of most other underdeveloped nations, China's economic progress during the last two decades must be regarded as astonishing. Epidemics and starvation, common in China before, are no more. China may no longer be described as *The Land of Famine*, the title of a missionary's book. The fact that she bought millions of tons of wheat from Australia and Canada had been used as evidence for the failure of Communism. But which pre-1949 Chinese government was interested enough in feeding its people to want to buy wheat abroad and could pay for it with cash?

For a visitor from the United States, it is easy enough to find economic shortcomings in today's China. She has no privately owned automobiles. Housing is not plentiful and people do live in crowded conditions. Luxury goods are scarce. Rice, pork, cloth, and some other food items such as bean curd are still rationed. Cigars, playing cards, and ham are available in some places, absent in others. Plumbing is only available in about 20 percent of the dwellings.

But even as early as 1955–57, and then in 1961 when I was traveling in India, I met scores of Indians who had visited China and told me how impressed they were by China's economic progress in comparison with India's. In those days, the key words among politically and socially active Indians was "development." And the one common answer I received when I asked why they were impressed by China was: "They have started to develop." This comparative perspective was probably what led Neville Maxwell, an English journalist and author of *India's China War,* reportedly to tell an American colleague that he must first visit India to appreciate what China has accomplished.

However, instead of following the Western route to industrialization, the Chinese plan is to combine industrialization with a new egalitarianism. And, instead of depending upon the self-seeking drives of the individualist, the Chinese look toward a group-oriented, almost altruistic man.

The new egalitarianism the Chinese are aiming at has many facets. It centers on the notion of "reducing distances" between those who use the mind and those who use the hand, between those on higher levels of the government and those on lower levels, between men and women, between party members and nonparty members, and between villages and cities.

On the surface there is, in China today, an apparent contradiction to this egalitarian goal, which is evident in one of the recurrent slogans, calling for "The Dictatorship of the Proletariat." Also, admission to schools of higher education is certainly biased against the children of those who formerly enjoyed capitalist or bureaucratic connections. The Chinese, however, consider this a transitional situation. Since private ownership of means of production has already been eliminated, everyone will have to be a proletarian. At that point, all Chinese will dictate over themselves.

The philosophy of egalitarianism is thoroughly Western. The Chinese philosophers spoke of "harmony of all under the heaven" but never equality of all under the heaven. For, ideologically, the traditional Chinese saw the world of man and of nature as hierarchical, albeit harmonious through hierarchy. However, the attributes of continuity and inclusiveness are such that de facto egalitarianism was not actually foreign to the Chinese reality.

For example, everywhere, people of high social status engage in conspicuous consumption to flaunt their status. However, instead of flaunting their status in an exclusive manner (such as moving to a restricted neighborhood or having only socially prominent guests in the house, etc.), wealthy Chinese used to do the opposite. They would have sumptuous weddings, funerals, and birthday celebrations to which they invited all the townspeople. In 1941, a prominent merchant family in West Town (my pseudonym for a small market town in Western Yunnan) invited all inhabitants within something like a 100 mile radius to come and participate in his father's funeral. He provided living quarters for all who came and extended to each his hospitality for a couple of days. To space out the guests, he announced a schedule in advance and posted it in the different villages and towns concerned. The funeral lasted a month. That was true expression of inclusiveness.

The Chinese admonition never to forget one's roots, was, of course, an expression of continuity. Even Chinese who became prominent or wealthy or both would never sever their links with their ancestral homes and graveyards which, in most instances, were in villages or small towns rather than in the capitals or cities where they worked. In fact, these Chinese would usually retire in the places of their origin. A prominent Chinese official could be a terror in the place of his appointment, but he would greatly enhance his prestige if he was kind and freely mingled with the people of his home village or town. That was an expression of inclusiveness as well.

The close ties between Chinese rural and urban areas were greatly loosened during the last hundred years under the impact of the West, with the intrusion of foreign concessions and Western styles of life that accentuated the differences between these areas and made the villages inferior places in which to live. The Communist government's plan of developing the cities without leaving the villages behind is, therefore, at least in a limited sense, a restoration of something traditionally Chinese and certainly does not conflict with it.

In the same vein sexual equality in the Chinese context does not present the problem it did and still does in the United States. Obviously, traditional Chinese institutions were male-centered. Henpecking stories notwithstanding, there was no question that husbands exercised authority over their wives as did brothers over sisters. However, when different generations are involved, we may find a situation like that of Chia Cheng in the *Dream of the Red Chamber,* who publicly subordinated himself to the power of his widowed mother. His masculinity was not threatened by such public acts of prostration; he was merely remaining conscious of his roots. By extension, the Chinese even had a proverb: "Older sister-in-law is like a mother." In other words, one should respect one's older brother's wife as one does his mother. In these matters traditional patterns of continuity and inclusiveness assist rather than present stumbling blocks to the goal of universal equality.

It was previously noted that the Chinese, eschewing the self-seeking drives of the individualist, instead, look toward a group oriented, almost altruistic man. This is a conscious goal China's new leaders hope to achieve, and slogans to that effect are common. The Chinese explain to visitors that many of their present-day activities are directed toward that goal. It was reported in the American press that when a group of visiting Chinese athletes in Europe were told about the great American feat of having landed the first men on the moon, the Chinese countered with the boast that they would put the first new men on earth. What is this new man or woman like? How do the Chinese hope to create him or her? How well are they succeeding?

I believe a central aspect in the creation of the new man or woman is found in Mao's slogan "Serve the People." That slogan is engraved on giant plaques installed in public places, on small badges worn by government functionaries and soldiers and workers alike, and is sewn on student bookbags.

To serve the people means, in the first place, carrying out one's duties faithfully and with good cheer. One expression of such cooperation was the snow removal scene in Peking during President Nixon's 1972 visit, which commentator Eric Sevareid described as totalitarianism in action. However, this is not exceptional. This care on the part of the ordinary worker for public property, from machinery to buildings, is apparent everywhere. The elevators in the best hotel for foreigners in Shanghai are each at least forty years old, and they still run perfectly. Workers in factories think of every conceivable way of increasing production and finding new uses for old wastes. Even the leftover skin, beard, and ashes of the wheat in a flour mill at Wuhan are, as Dick and Eileen report, now made into medicine for scabies.

The reader will find numerous other examples of what the Chinese mean by serving the people. But how does one maximize the spirit of serving the people? The answer is, *hsueh hsi*, or study sessions. The members of every work unit, whether factory, school, commune, bank, or government office, participate regularly in such sessions at least twice a week, in some instances more. They may take place during work hours or in the evenings.

The common outsider's view of such sessions is that they are indoctrination classes where the participants take in varying doses of works by Marx, Lenin, and Mao. While that is largely true, it is rarely pointed out that these are also occasions when the lofty theories are related to practices at hand.

I asked Comrade Sung, one of the young ladies who was our waitress at the Chien Men Hotel in Peking for eighteen days, to tell me some of her gains in the study sessions.

It so happened that a few days before this conversation I had seen Chinese firepots being enjoyed by other guests in the dining room. Since we always had firepots during Chinese New Year celebrations in my parents' home in Manchuria where I grew up, I was interested in comparing the kind of ingredients I knew years ago with what the hotel served now. When I asked Comrade Sung about this, it turned out she could only mention a few items and did not know the rest.

Now she put it this way in answer to my query about the study sessions: "For example, the other day you (using the polite form *nin*) asked me about firepot ingredients and I could not name them satisfactorily. So during one of our study sessions, when one comrade spoke on the subject of how to improve our services, I offered my inability to answer your question as illustration. Now, not only have I gone back and memorized all the ingredients for the firepot but, in view of my admission, others have also found some ways of improving their services."

But study sessions involve more than self-criticism. Each participant may and should criticize others on any relevant subject. On the first day, when we visited my mother-in-law and her family in Wuhan, an endless stream of visitors from the neighborhood came to say hello and to see Eileen and her younger sister Penny, whose long hair aroused endless comments and curiosity everywhere. The head of the Street Revolutionary Committee came as did a teacher of one of my brother-in-law's daughters. The teacher stayed longest, over an hour, conversing with my wife and two daughters. All in all it was an exhausting, noisy, but exhilarating occasion, full of people coming and going and full of simultaneous conversations.

To our surprise, six weeks later, when my mother-in-law and my brother-in-law came to spend a week with us in Shanghai, my brother-in-law told me that the teacher was subsequently criticized in a study session for staying so long. She was called "selfish" and "inconsiderate" on two grounds: she took up too much of the time our relatives might have liked to spend alone with us; and she gave other neighbors and friends less opportunity to greet the visitors.

I relate these seemingly minor incidents, the one concerning the firepot and the other, visiting too long—not to detract from the importance of the study sessions, but to indicate their broad scope. Of course, weighty matters are also considered in these sessions, from class struggle to the Paris Commune and what lessons the latter holds for China. But no subject is too small for review. In this way, a link is developed between national goal and personal conduct, and everyone has a sense of participation.

Contrary to popular impressions, this link is not a one-way route, with the lower echelons passively taking orders from the higher ones. That negative connotation arose because of misinterpretation of terms like "brain washing" and "thought reform," very much identified in the West with Chinese Communism when it first took power. Brain washing and thought reform are common processes in all education, reeducation, propaganda, or advertising. When American schools introduce new math and sex education and attempt to inform the students of the consequences of drug abuse, they are doing nothing short of brain washing or thought reform. Politicians try to brainwash their constituents when they deliberately cultivate an image of progressiveness or incorruptibility. Liberals hope to do nothing less than thought reform when they endeavor to disabuse people of racial or religious prejudice. And the brainwashing power of advertisement is all too well known to need elaboration.

Of course, the new Chinese government hopes to achieve a great deal of psychological change in the society as a whole, but the process for this change is a two-way interaction of stimulus and response. The overall goal of the party is the building of a socialist society, a goal no more negotiable than is the goal of the Catholic church. But how best to build that socialist society is the concern of every Chinese. The average Chinese worker, farmer, or soldier expresses his or her views by his reactions (*fan ying*) to directives from his leaders as well as by his reactions to reality as seen by the way he performs his tasks.

During the 1972 Nixon visit to China, American reporters were very disappointed when they tried to interview some Chinese men on the street as they were accustomed to doing in their own country. They thought the Chinese were not informed and did not care about the visit. I cannot say whether that was true as far as the few Chinese interviewed were concerned. But, what I learned

in China a few months later was that the idea of a Nixon visit was very much the subject of study sessions long before the American President's arrival.

It is probably not likely that, in an event of such importance, the workers, farmers, and soldiers in study sessions could have prevented the visit from taking place should their *fan ying* to it be adverse. But the fact that they were given a chance to discuss it in advance cannot but further the link between the individual and the larger political society. We should not lose sight of the meaning of that link simply because, in this case, a contrary *fan ying* in the study sessions could not have reversed the higher decision, any more than we should minimize the power of the American people over their government just because their elected representatives in Washington, D.C., had for so long failed to stop their President from continuing the Vietnam War.

In America many stores, factories, and institutions have provisions for customer complaints or employee grievances. The complaints or grievances are adjusted generally in terms of personal or group injuries and dissatisfactions. That is to say, when a customer gets his defective merchandise replaced or an undutiful employee is punished, that is the end of the matter. In addition, the Better Business Bureau, Better Government Association, television or radio stations that assist listeners and viewers, and Nader's organizations all play a part in securing consumer justice or cutting bureaucratic red tape. But the overriding aim of all this is to redress certain wrongs and protect the ordinary consumer or little man from present or possible future wrongs. They may expose in the process the means by which the wrongs were committed or perpetrated and discuss new legislation to prevent their recurrence, but as a rule these measures do not lead to discussion of the basic principles whereby such wrongs thrive.

In the Chinese scene, on the other hand, every complaint tends to be tied to the discussion of some weighty principles of Maoist socialism. We went to the wrong pier in Shanghai to receive our relatives who came by boat from Wuhan. Its gatekeeper was both impatient and unhelpful toward us and our China Travel Service guide. He simply said something to the effect that "this is not it. . . . I don't know which is the right pier," and then he waved to us not to bother him. That was the only time we met with such rudeness.

Instead of becoming angry, our guide told us he would send his reaction (*fan ying fan ying**) to his superiors and the latter would ask the culprit's superior to make his misconduct a subject for a study session in the culprit's work unit. "The trouble," Comrade Hwang concluded, "is some of us don't really understand the meaning of Chairman Mao's 'serve the people'."

The link between everyday conduct and higher principles is so much a part of Chinese consciousness today that an appeal to these principles can usually resolve interpersonal difficulties. One of our drivers in Wuhan was a daredevil on wheels. Feeling uncomfortable with his several near misses, I gently reminded him that accidents surely would not help him in building a socialist society. He slowed down considerably after that. In one of the only two public altercations I witnessed in the streets of Shanghai, a policeman intervened by touching the arm of the more vociferous of the combatants and said: "Comrade, regardless of the merits of the case, your attitude toward the other comrade is unbecoming." And that led to an apology from the man and an end to the affair.

Next to serving the people, the Chinese new man should shun elitism. The idea of nonelitism, while closely related, and in fact instrumental to egalitarianism, is not identical with it. American society is egalitarian but elitist. That is, everyone, in principle at least, has the opportunity to achieve. However, those who do take advantage of the opportunity and succeed, are, even in principle, no longer the equals of those who have lagged behind.

The Chinese idea is quite different. As a means of achieving ultimate equality for all, the present leadership discriminates against those from privileged backgrounds. That is why children of the formerly affluent are not easily admitted to institutions of higher learning. Similarly, in America, today, people have claimed there is reverse discrimination in the black-white situation. I have more than once heard from young white Americans seeking college admission that they suffer from their whiteness. In both societies, the situation is presumed to be temporary. But what distinguishes the Chinese social design is that equality must prevail regardless of achievement, that all individual superiority, for any reason, is to be eliminated. Specialization, yes. Some specializations are more complicated and require more training and learning, but superiority, no. The Chinese hope to create a nation of workers, farmers, and soldiers while the Americans still claim everyone can be president.

Chinese education on all levels emphasizes the importance of the smarter and the quicker of mind helping the dull and the less intelligent. Children do homework together. They exchange solutions to problems freely. For, the theme is "we advance together."

Another way of discouraging elitism is for the more educated to work side by side with the less educated, for the intellectuals and government officials to work on cotton gins, press oil in factories, feed pigs, or plant rice on farms. All graduates from junior high (the end of compulsory education) must do manual work for a minimum of two years before hoping for a chance of higher education. Entrance into college and the attainment of professional ranks (such as doctor or dentist) are not the end of manual work. All students and their teachers reside and work on farms for at least one month a year. When temporary labor is urgently needed at harvest times, a common sight is that of marching students with their teachers coming from all over to assist on the farms. In this way, the Chinese hope not merely to shorten the material distance between the cities and the villages, but also to build and maintain a strong psychological bridge between them.

---

*"React react." In everyday conversation the Chinese language is replete with repetition of the same verb to give emphasis. Other examples, "see see," "smell smell."

I noted with interest a recent newspaper report about a new prep school, under the principalship of a 37-year-old educator, that will have a city campus in Chicago as well as a 320-acre farm campus in Wisconsin. Each pupil will live and work on the farm for three ten-day periods during the fall, winter, and spring. Characteristically, as the educator explains it, this new school hopes to solve the problem that "most kids are bored most of the time in most schools."

In a similar vein, there was another news report about a college president who spent a two-month vacation "digging ditches, collecting garbage and washing dishes." He learned, in the end, that "people do work hard . . . and they work harder when there is a meaningful job to do, and if they feel appreciated."

While both American experiments may bear some resemblance to the Chinese work-study program for creating new men, that resemblance is more superficial than substantive. The urban school with a country campus is designed to motivate its students to acquire "the necessary skills for success on a variety of standardized measures." As for the college president, he really learned nothing new. Surely he knew before his adventure that people "work harder where there is a meaningful job to do, and if they feel appreciated." Who wouldn't? But, is a "meaningful job" being a sandwich man or a ditch digger for $2.75 an hour in a highly competitive society, where others make millions for far less physical exertion and flaunt it ostentatiously? How will these workers "feel appreciated"?

It is precisely this sense of meaningfulness to be derived from whatever task one is responsible for that the Chinese hope to cultivate in their new man. That is what the study sessions and the concept of serving the people are all about. But study sessions and leadership from above can only assist toward achieving the desired goal. There are two other factors of even greater importance. One is a political economy which allows no great disparity in individual income and no significant private ownership of means of production. The other is the Chinese pattern of mutual dependence

among men. In both of these, China and America differ profoundly.

What is obvious is that, where there is no great difference in income and little private ownership, a major source of human friction is absent. Edgar Snow expounded this point very eloquently.

> Many crimes have ceased, according to Mr. Wu (Judge Wu Teh-fang, chairman of politics and law), simply because of the elimination of private estate ownership. I thought of this while I was marooned by floods in a small Manchurian town where I found in a hotel library two volumes of Sherlock Holmes stories. After reading them all I went back over the plots and confirmed an impression: without exception, every murder or *crime passionnel* solved by the master mind of Baker Street was directly or indirectly motivated by greed or covetousness [*The Other Side of the River* (New York: Random House 1961), p. 355].

Those to whom private property is sacred may retort, we can't throw out the baby with the bath water, or ask sarcastically whether the way to stop highway slaughter is to eliminate travel. This essay is not a sermon. It merely explains the differing conditions which seem to affect human behavior. If we don't wish to stop travel altogether, can we at least ask, whether all those trips are necessary? The lack of private ownership of property has certainly seemed to affect Chinese behavior. It is an established fact that gangsters and racketeers have disappeared in China. It is also known that, in contrast to the situation in the United States, litigation is rare in China today. "There is no backlog of cases and courts are recessed for days at a time because of no business. . . . Shanghai was the first place I managed to find a court in session and was able to hear a trial" (Snow, p. 355).

The cultural pattern of mutual dependence is the final ingredient that makes China's new man possible. It forms the foundation of the way the Chinese individual feels about himself, relates to others and to the rest of the world. And this foundation is greatly strengthened by economic equality. Elsewhere I explained mutual dependence extensively [Francis L. K. Hsu, *Americans and Chinese: Purpose and Fulfillment in Great Civilizations* (New York: Doubleday, 1970)]. Briefly, it is this. Personal fulfillment, as well as social esteem, for the Chinese has always been based on how well a person has functioned as son, father, and friend. This includes, by extension, bringing honor and prosperity to one's kin and local community. An unfilial Chinese, no matter how great his official or scholarly achievement, was invariably vilified by his biographers.

Consequently, the Chinese individual thought nothing of inviting others to help out with his domestic difficulties or his personal shortcomings, and he tended to be far more willing to enter into the personal affairs of his relatives, friends, and neighbors. Privacy, as understood by Americans, was nonexistent, and calling someone a loner (*tu* or *tu jen*) is still equivalent to branding him as selfish. Within the Chinese kinship and local group, there was a sense of interrelatedness and mutual interest, unknown by their American counterparts. The Chinese pattern did not work perfectly, of course, any more than did the Christian ideal of love thy neighbor or the American pattern of individual self-reliance, with its corollaries freedom and equality. Problems in China and in the West abound. But each overall cultural orientation and their differing points of emphasis were unmistakable.

Given that Chinese pattern, the son's gain was not the father's loss. Nor was the nephew's gain his uncle's loss. The attributes of continuity and inclusiveness minimized the chances of such interpersonal rivalry and envy. The new government in China has simply tried to build a new national corporation on the basis of the traditional Chinese pattern of mutual dependence. Toward this end, it has reduced (but not eliminated) the sphere of influence of kinship and local groups by initiating a whole series of new organizations: street revolutionary committees, communes, factories, Chairman Mao propaganda teams, May Seventh Cadre Schools, and new universities in which students, faculty, clerks and janitors, Party members, People's Liberation Army (PLA) soldiers, all have a voice. They have created new art and literature to promote the new objectives. They have moved many men and women from one region to another, or from more accessible places to less accessible ones.

I well remember the difficulties my friends and I encountered in the 30s in Shanghai and Canton, where the dialects are foreign to us. Now I found that the local inhabitants all command a sort of *Pu tung hwa* (common speech) as well as their native dialects. In addition, I found many hotel clerks, merchants, and government functionaries from other parts of the country. One of my most fruitful conversations was with a young clerk in the Canton hotel on our way out. He happened to be a native of Chin Chow in eastern Manchuria, where I spent a good many of my pre-teen and teen years. We talked about familiar places, compared our experiences growing up.

But the new and greatly expanded organizations are founded on the same old Chinese notion that man does not stand alone, that he can only better himself and the world around him through cooperation with his fellow man, and through the linkage of different generations. In other words, what the Chinese are trying to achieve is continuity and inclusiveness in a greatly expanded human sphere: instead of continuity and inclusiveness of the kinship and local groups, they must now be extended to include the nation as a whole.

I think this sense of interrelatedness at every level provides a better condition under which human beings can find their jobs "meaningful" and feel themselves "appreciated" and thus, according to the adventurous American college president, "work harder."

This, too, in my view is the point that Mao tries to convey to his followers when he related the old Chinese story of "The Foolish Old Man Who Plans to Move a Mountain." The old man was ridiculed when he began the task. But he replied, "I may not be able to get rid of it in my lifetime, but my sons and my sons' sons will continue the effort after I die. The mountain will not grow but my descendants will." The foolish old man's view is, in turn, thoroughly consonant with the Chinese solution to the myth of the Primeval Flood we noted before.

The attribute of authority runs through all of this, from the study sessions to the prevention of elitism, from the concept of serving the people to the sense of continuity between the generations. During the height of the Cultural Revolution, some China Watchers had opined that the rampaging Red Guards were part of a worldwide rising tide of the young against the old. I think that observation as worthless as another which saw China returning to the chaotic days of the warlords. The Red Guard movement was instigated from the top. The Chinese youngsters did not look, as would many individualist Americans, to their own conscience for guidance. Instead, they brandished and closely followed what was propounded in Mao's "little red book." When the highest authority of the land decided it was enough, they were stopped with relative speed. Could the American government call off student demonstrations or youthful misconduct as easily? Now, three years after the Cultural Revolution, several university professors told us they wished their students were less passive in their learning habits. The Chinese never had the notion of bucking authority for the sake of it. They rebel only when authority is too oppressive or when it does not function.

At the beginning of this essay, we referred to four Chinese attributes as keys to understanding China: continuity, inclusiveness, authority, and asexuality. Although we have so far not dealt with the attribute of asexuality in analyzing China's post-1949 developments, the only differences to be found today are the elimination of some of the age old frills and abuses of sex resulting from social inequality. Otherwise, the Chinese new men have not moved far from the customary Chinese pattern of understatement.

One of the slogans of the May Fourth Movement (1919) led by Dr. Hu Shih of Peking University was *yi ku* (doubt old). For some years afterwards an auxiliary slogan was *ta tao Kung chia tien* (down with Confucius store). There is no question that some of the new goals and usages such as prevention of elitism and physical labor for the highly educated are aimed at negating a fundamental tenet of Confucius: "Who works with his mind rules; who works with his hand is ruled." However, I cannot help but note the basic similarity between what the Chinese are trying to do today and the social ideal in Confucian thought over twenty centuries ago:

> When the Great Tao is realized, all is for all's sake. . . . We hate to see any goods left wasted. There is no need for private ownership. As for strength in our bodies, we hate to see it unused. There is no need for individual service. Thus we have no ground for craftiness, jealousy and corruption. This is what we call the Great Communal Good [*Li Yun* Section, *Li Chi*].

It is still too early to tell to what extent the Chinese have achieved their goal of creating this new man. Nevertheless, we were able to make certain observations which have been corroborated by other visitors. There is little crime, and no personal violence. Services are generally excellent in spite of the abolition of tips. There is an extraordinary camaraderie between the brain workers and manual workers, and there is freedom from bureaucratic corruption. We noticed among workers a zeal for duty and for the protection of public property. But is there not more discontent than appears on the surface in China today? As industrialization advances and life's amenities become more plentiful, will the pressure for elitism not increase? Have we visitors been "put on" by the Chinese we have met? Time alone will tell. I hardly think so.

How much can visitors from America learn about China when the two social systems are so different? Are they not subject to the danger of overgeneralizing?

For example, some readers of my book *Americans and Chinese* have criticized me for attributing to Americans greater uniformity than they actually possess, considering the diversity of their ethnic origins. My answer to that criticism is that it depends on the level of our generalizations. Read a book such as *Honor Thy Father,* and we at once realize there are great differences within the United States. However, let an American go to Vietnam, as a soldier or civilian, he will most assuredly encounter Vietnamese patterns of behavior and personal relationships that are totally alien to him. Their sense of time is not the same as his. They do not care about dogs the way he does. They tend more to mix sentiment with business. And, while there is official corruption amongst both groups, its manifestations differ.

For instance, in the United States, whoever pays the bill calls the tune. When someone pays money to an official or contributes to his campaign, he expects to gain some control in return. But in Vietnam, as in traditional China, the officials are on top. You pay because you owe it to them, and it is for the officials to determine whether or not they want to do you a favor. These sorts of differences are very obvious to most or all Americans dealing with Vietnam, regardless of their ethnic or geographical origin. However, observers on all sides must realize at what level their generalizations are valid and make no excessive claims.

No visitor to any place can claim to know everything about that place or even everything about a particular aspect of that place simply because he has been there. In fact, no native can make that claim either. Do Chicagoans know everything that goes on in Chicago? Why are those sordid details of the Watergate mess that are unfolding before the public still so unbelievable to some Americans? Do Texans really know what was behind the Kennedy assassination?

Even in the People's Republic today, monolithic as it may seem, there is variation from area to area. The hotel services are best in Peking, not so good in Canton. Ladies' dresses are more stylish in Shanghai. We even saw three or four young girls with miniskirts. Shenyang (Mukden) obviously has less sartorial elegance. Our visit occurred in the summer months. We are sure that winter clothing is bound to be more somber.

One learned white American couple told us after their China visit how much they were impressed by the Chinese pride in "being Chinese." "They say the Chinese are a yellow race," the couple told us, "but we have never seen more red cheeked faces anywhere as we have in China. They are so proud of being Chinese." I think this couple was merely seeing the Chinese situation in an American context. The Chinese are not simply proud of being Chinese in the way American blacks are proud of being black in a society dominated by whites. In the normal course of events, the Chinese in China see only other Chinese, and, only rarely, foreigners. These Chinese are proud of how China has moved as a nation. Even old women with bound feet and old men requiring canes for walking have stood up and acknowledged pride in the nation for what it has done, rather than pride in themselves for being Chinese.

The particular developmental period of China may make a great deal of difference in what the visitor can or cannot see. For example, in the 50s and early 60s, a number of foreign visitors including Dr. Gregorio Bermann of Argentina visited a number of psychiatric hospitals and clinics in Canton, Peking, Shanghai, and Nanking [see Gregorio Bermann, "Mental Health in China" in *Psychiatry in the Communist World,* ed. Ari Kiev (New York: Science House, 1968), pp. 223-61]. That was, however, before the Cultural Revolution of 1966–68. In the summer of 1972, although we tried, we were unable to be shown a psychiatric hospital anywhere. Could it be that the Chinese authorities were still fearful that some visitors might, without good foundation, mistake some of the cases of mental illness for the deleterious effects of the Cultural Revolution? We did not know.

As Eileen and Dick explain in the book, Chinese visitors could enter China as *hua chiao* (overseas chinese) or as *wai bin* (foreign guest). Generally the two groups are put up in separate hotels and taken care of by different travel bureaus. We went as wai bin, and some of the experiences of our friends and acquaintances who went as hua chiao sometimes differed from ours.

Finally, even the five of us touring China together could not but have some unlike experiences. My wife and I were born and raised in China. We know a lot about China before 1949, and we have perfect command of the language. We were old-timers returning home, so to speak. Eileen and her younger sister Penny were born and raised in the United States. They could not but have been imbued with some Chinese attributes and feelings about things, because my wife and I raised them. But their Chinese is less fluent, they had no Chinese schooling, and they have, for most of their lives, associated with white Americans rather than Chinese since we do not live in Chinatown. They are Americans in most senses of the word. Dick is a native American, born and raised on Long Island and educated in eastern schools. He had no Chinese experience and little knowledge about the country except through his marriage to Eileen and what, despite his usual American objection to any parental authority, rubbed off his parents-in-law.

It is not surprising that while in China, we disagreed occasionally about our observations. For example, Dick and Eileen found photographing people in China extremely difficult. As soon as a camera was revealed, the people would disperse or hide their faces. Once, while Dick was shooting pictures a teenager came forward and covered the camera lens with his palm. On the other hand, once or twice people dispersed when they saw me taking out my camera, but generally my experiences were quite different from theirs. I always found a brief get-acquainted conversation with the prospective subject or subjects very helpful. In fact, a number of times mothers held up their babies for me to photograph, and, after their babies were photographed, they allowed me to photograph themselves. Teenagers volunteered as subjects until I had more than I could handle. The Chinese like to be photographed in formal poses, with several subjects standing in a row or two. It recalls the older Chinese portraits in which even a single subject must be flanked by potted flowers and a side table with a clock. But a brief explanation of what I wanted usually got my way.

Then Eileen noted that, in the dining room at the border station where we entered China, we were seated halfway between the foreigners and some Chinese workers who were having their lunch. Eileen at once thought there was some symbolic meaning to this. My wife and I did not even recall this seating arrangement. In fact, as we now reflect on it, we still think we were put at the end of the dining room not far from the kitchen because the waitresses wanted to talk to us. One waitress talked to us a lot, especially about the long hair of our two girls. When my wife told her the trouble she had in getting our girls to agree to cut their hair shorter, the waitress even lectured them jokingly on how daughters should obey their mothers. We learned a great deal about her family, her marriage, and her work.

What all this says is that each observer, native or foreign, can only see a segment of reality, inevitably colored by his or her background and previous experiences. We can only approach the truth by observing the same event from different angles aided by observers of diverse backgrounds.

It is hoped this book will make a substantial contribution to this end. The writer of an introduction to a book normally praises the book. But here I am very much up against my Chinese up-bringing. Embodying the attributes of continuity but especially inclusiveness, I feel that Eileen's and Dick's book is also mine. Therefore, praising their book is like blowing my own horn.

So even though I am sure the reader will find much enjoyment in the following pages and learn a great deal about life in China today from them, I must underplay my enthusiasm and tell the reader:

This is not a bad book. My children have tried their best.

Evanston, Illinois   FRANCIS L. K. HSU

PRELUDE

My family and I did not travel as *hua ch'iao* (overseas Chinese), but rather, as foreigners (*wai pin*). There are advantages to both forms, but we had no choice. We were told that, if we went as hua ch'iao, Dick could not travel with us in the event that his visa came through.

Foreigners have passports and visas. Hua ch'iao have special papers issued to them in Hong Kong. Every person of Chinese ancestry is eligible to apply as a hua ch'iao, while all other foreigners may apply for visas at the nearest Chinese embassy as wai pin. Most Chinese apply as hua ch'iao.

Foreigners are supposed to make travel arrangements, which must be approved in advance, listing each town they plan to visit and how long they intend to stay. Hua ch'iao need only say where they are going next, with no time restrictions for each stop (within the limits of their permit for total stay in China). The only requirement is that their travel document be stamped when they arrive in and leave each town. (There are areas where no non-Chinese citizen can go, hua ch'iao or foreign.)

The China International Travel Service, for foreigners, and the Hua Ch'iao Travel Service are completely separate organizations. They have different guides and use different hotels, although there are occasional substitutions.

The guides who work for the Hua Ch'iao Travel Service speak only Chinese, and the forms that hua ch'iao must fill out are in Chinese. After receiving their papers, hua ch'iao leave Hong Kong for the Chinese border on the 7:30 A.M. train. When they arrive, they are led to an area with wooden benches where Chinese customs agents examine their luggage in minute detail. Friends of ours who traveled as hua ch'iao reported that cosmetic bottles were opened, and all newspapers and other printed matter were taken away.

We, as foreigners, had first-class accommodations on the 9:30 A.M. train from Hong Kong to the border. Our baggage, wooden benches downstairs. After passing a giant photograph of Chairman Mao surrounded by smiling Asian and African faces (including Malcolm X), we were separated into several groups, each in a different waiting room with ceiling fan, soft chairs, a tea thermos, and a rack of Chinese magazines and little red books printed in many languages and free for the taking. There weren't any in Chinese.

One by one, the people in the room were taken away to customs. Only hua ch'iao are allowed to bring extra items as gifts for relatives, which is one reason their luggage is checked so thoroughly. They sometimes sneak things like watches into the country and sell them. We, as foreigners, were not entitled to bring gifts, since we were not supposed to have relatives there. The customs agent decided to treat us as hua ch'iao as far as gifts were concerned, and as foreigners in every other regard. He glanced at the watches, cloth, and other items we had brought for our relatives and also looked at our film. Upon opening my suitcase, he gave it only a cursory look. We were permitted to keep our printed matter.

After changing some money at the bank, we were then taken to yet another room to rest—more stuffed chairs, a balcony with a grape arbor and jasmine plants. We were called to lunch. Hua ch'iao have the option of buying lunch, while lunch for foreigners is included in the price of the train ticket. The dining room featured two old still lifes at one end and purple velvet curtains over the doorways. The seating was arranged by nationality. At separate tables were: six Japanese businessmen, a black man, three German businessmen, a Pakistani, and a Sikh and an Englishwoman representing the United Kingdom. My family was seated at a table in the middle of the dining room, and we immediately began a friendly conversation with the waitress.

After more waiting, we boarded the train for Canton. The hua ch'iao rode in cars at the rear of the train, with foreigners together in front. When the girl came to take my family's tickets, she said *kippu,* which is Japanese for ticket. Some Chinese were still assuming that we were not Chinese. Per-

Shanghai

bearing white tags with a red star in the middle, disappeared at the Hong Kong train station. After an hour's ride we arrived at Lo Wu, the border. Once through Hong Kong immigration, past the Union Jack and the British soldiers with machine guns, we crossed a bridge where we met the Chinese People's Liberation Army (PLA) and their machine guns. They checked our papers and led us, with the other foreigners, into a waiting room filled with upholstered chairs. Soldiers, who spoke various languages, came around to look at our health cards. They assumed my family and I were not Chinese, and they addressed us in English.

We were then led to another building while music played. On our way upstairs we passed a large white statue of Chairman Mao with a red flag behind it and caught a glimpse of the hua ch'iao waiting on their haps this was because most hua ch'iao who come to China are from Southeast Asia and dress accordingly, while most oriental visitors wearing Western clothes are from Japan.

In Canton we were accidentally booked into the hua ch'iao hotel and assigned hua ch'iao guides. The mixup was resolved, however, when we went to the foreigners' hotel but kept the hua ch'iao guide. I can only report on the hua ch'iao hotels by telling what I have been told by Chinese who stayed there. The quality was variable. The rooms were less expensive than the foreigners' rooms, costing on the average a few dollars per day, as opposed to ten to fifteen dollars. In small towns, foreigners and hua ch'iao stayed in the same hotels.

We encountered one indication of official flexibility when we requested that a girlfriend of mine, traveling as a hua ch'iao, be permitted to travel with us. Permission was granted, although people in Hong Kong had told us it would never be allowed.

Although conditions in each town varied, in general, taxis were not as readily available at hua ch'iao hotels as they were at foreigners' hotels. Partly, this is because hua ch'iao speak Chinese and can take public transportation. Foreigners are assumed incapable of negotiating the buses and trolleys.

However, differential treatment extended to the sightseeing as well. Hua ch'iao generally went in groups, on buses, even if they had not come to China as a group. If foreigners were not members of an official group they went sightseeing in individual cars, with a private guide. I went to see the Great Wall twice, once as a foreigner and once as a hua ch'iao. As foreigners, it cost my family $25 to go in a private car, without a guide. As hua ch'iao it cost Dick and me $14, or $7 each, to go on a bus. This last fee included a box lunch.

Traveling first with my family and then alone with Dick gave me some insight into Chinese behavior toward foreigners. Although we were well-treated as a family, some people seemed more willing to extend themselves when Dick and I were alone. Buses made special stops for us, and we

were not asked to show our identification to gain admission to the various Friendship Stores, where only people with foreign passports are admitted. In Shanghai, for example, the Friendship Store is filled with luxury items including old art objects and traditional Chinese furniture and porcelain. It has a separate building in which one can find Chinese-made watches, musical instruments, cosmetics, and clothing and cloth in styles and colors unavailable in ordinary stores. When my family and I went, we had to show our passports. Dick, on the other hand, was simply able to walk in. Frankly, in several cases his face elicited prompter, more courteous service.

This service difference was also noticeable at the Bank of China and at the post office where foreigners were immediately taken care of, no matter how many other people might be waiting. When my family and I went with our guide, we too received preferential treatment.

At one point in Peking I wanted to buy some children's clothes for friends in America. In order to buy cotton clothing one needs ration tickets, which I didn't have, but ordinarily, if you explain that you are a foreigner, there is no further problem. However, this particular store refused to sell the outfits to me, with the manager ex-

Pataling

Sian

Sian

plaining nicely that only foreigners could buy without ration tickets. I offered to show him my passport, but he said it wouldn't make any difference. In another Peking store I had no difficulty in purchasing similar outfits. Dick never experienced any problems of this type. Several other stores I visited in Peking had special sections behind curtains which only foreigners could enter. One was a rug store, another a secondhand store. I was with several white people, so I don't know if I could have entered had I been alone. We saw old silk clothing and more art objects.

When it came time to leave China, the difference between foreigner and hua ch'iao persisted up to the border. Foreigners could take out undeveloped film, but hua ch'iao had to have theirs developed. While foreigners were allowed to change any unused Chinese currency back into Hong Kong dollars, hua ch'iao had to exchange theirs for goods worth, in general, slightly less than the currency. Our suitcases were not even opened, whereas hua ch'iao luggage was carefully examined.

The two groups rode the same train, but separate cars, back to the border. This time the foreigners' car was air conditioned. Once over the border on the Hong Kong side, we waited for the train back to the city. It was the first time in three months that I had to wait for anything on a hard wooden bench, outside, with everyone else. Instead of the ubiquitous tea, little children were selling coca-cola.

This preferential treatment for foreign guests is quite pervasive. If a foreigner walks into a store, the lights go on and the fans start turning. Four salesmen will immediately come over. While, on the one hand, this treatment is very gratifying, it is, at the same time, somewhat reminiscent of colonial days. This is, of course, not their intention—the Chinese are trying to be courteous to their guests. However, the result is that most foreigners are effectively isolated from unofficial Chinese people.

Most foreigners visiting China eat all their meals in their hotels. When they go to a restaurant, they usually call ahead, and a special room is reserved so that, if they eat with anyone, it is with other foreigners. At the theater, for another example, foreign guests often are timed to arrive after everyone else has been seated, and the audience applauds as the guests file in. This is somewhat confusing and embarrassing, since one has done nothing to deserve such treatment. Also, although they are applauding, the audience usually has not been told who the guests are. To make matters worse, during intermissions we were sometimes led away to a private room to relax and be served tea and soft drinks. After the performance the audience was occasionally held back physically to allow the foreigners to leave first. At a volleyball game in Sian I heard the announcer tell the crowd several times not to leave before we did.

These efforts, intended as a demonstration of courtesy, made me very uncomfortable. In a society trying very hard to make everyone equal for the first time, who were we to be treated so deferentially? Other visitors may like this treatment—I did not.

We saw relatives in several towns I visited with my parents: Wuhan, Tientsin, Shenyang, and Shanghai. The China Travel Service guide was advised, in advance of our arrival, of the names of our relatives and where we thought they were living. In every instance our relatives were waiting for us at the train station or airport when we arrived. Transportation was arranged for them by the Travel Service. My grandmother, who did not notify the Travel Service that she was going to the airport, was driven there by one of my uncles who borrowed a jeep from work.

Without exception, the authorities bent over backward to allow our relatives to be with us. We had total privacy, and our relatives ate with us in the hotels. In Shenyang my cousin, his wife, and his daughter were invited to stay in our hotel and eat with us at government expense. In Shanghai, when my grandmother and one uncle came to visit us for a week, they were allowed to stay with us in the fanciest foreigners' hotel because of my grandmother's age (78). We visited relatives in their homes, and these visits were cleared in advance with the Revolutionary Committee of each Street Association. Sometimes during our visits a steady stream of neighbors would come to be introduced and refuse our offer of some candy especially purchased for our visit, until finally it was forced into their hands.

Our close relatives (uncles, aunts, cousins) were given time off from work to be with us. Cousins who were working far away were excused to come home to be with us for the length of our stay. My uncle's factory in Wuhan gave him leave when we came to Wuhan, and again when we asked him to accompany my grandmother to Shanghai.

In several instances we visited my relatives' places of work. We went to both uncles' companies in Wuhan, neither of which was accustomed to visitors. We later heard that one, a flour mill, had cut down a tree to provide a parking area for our cars. The other, a construction company, had whitewashed one room, transforming it into a reception room, and then purchased a new set of teacups. We were the first visitors at the flour mill since a Russian expert had come to inspect it many years ago, and we were the first foreigners ever to visit the construction company.

In Tientsin we went with our relatives to the cemetery where my father's brother is buried. Actually the place is a crematorium, open since 1955. It is located in the middle of an old graveyard, with hillocks of dusty earth, dry grass, and old gravestones scattered around. We parked near a group of brick buildings and showed the caretaker a card with a number on it. He took us to a room containing many wooden shelves, each filled with boxes of ashes. The boxes were the size of a woman's jewelry box. Most had pictures of the deceased on them, and each was elaborately decorated. Even though there is a general campaign against "superstition," a room is provided to which the box may be taken by people wishing to make food or wine offerings. On the walls were posters explaining why cremation is more sanitary and convenient than burial. Further, although the burning of paper money in the form of ingots or coins, another old "superstition," is officially discouraged, there is a pavilion available

Shanghai

outside where offerings may be burned. We burned some paper money that we had made the night before. The remains of many other paper offerings were apparent.

On our way out we passed a funeral. The mourners had come with the body and a paper wreath on a truck. The truck rental and cremation cost $8, three years storage of the ashes cost 75¢, and the death certificate, 4¢. The mourners were wearing black armbands. Some wore white caps and white shirts or jackets or white headbands with a red ball in the center of the forehead. Many were crying.

We went into the farewell room they had just vacated. Lined with wreaths from many funerals, it had a blue counter at one end, and behind the counter an empty space, then curtains and a hospital stretcher. The body is brought from the truck to behind the counter, where the mourners say farewell. Then the body is taken to the crematorium and the mourners leave. They later receive a notice in the mail telling them the box number of the ashes.

It is difficult to take photographs in China for several reasons. In the first place, the Chinese do not like strangers to photograph them in casual poses. When Dick would come upon someone unaware of his presence, another person would usually run up to the subject and tell him that he was being photographed. This is one reason you rarely see good, unposed close-up pictures from China, except those taken with a long lens. Secondly, almost immediately after a foreigner steps onto the street a huge crowd, often 100 people, forms around him. Not only is it difficult to photograph through such a crowd, but its presence makes the photographer conspicuous. Often Dick would simply have to leave the area. Once he walked out of a park, followed by a group. He then walked right back in, leaving the group outside, because, unlike him, they had to buy tickets again to reenter.

What interests these crowds more than anything else is foreign clothing. We overheard many comments, especially regarding our shoes. Should a foreigner enter a

Canton: reacting to a camera

Shanghai

Shanghai: Post Office

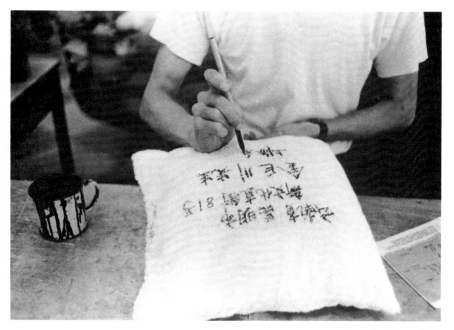

Shanghai: Post Office

store, so will the crowd. Should he get into a car, the crowd will press up to the windows. We once had to close a window in a dining room to avoid being watched while we ate, only to have someone outside immediately open it up again.

This staring is another reason the Chinese try to protect foreigners from exposure. There are people posted at hotel entrances to keep the general population out. Nevertheless, in some places, many neighborhood people bring their stools and their children to spend a pleasant summer evening sitting across the street from a hotel being entertained by the foreigners going in and out.

Staring is not a recent development. My parents recall having done some staring themselves when they were children in China. It is also very common in other parts of the world where outsiders are uncommon. The only time we were not stared at in public came during our visit to the Peking Zoo, when there was general hilarity over a chimpanzee who was spitting his urine at the crowd around his cage. Our act paled by comparison.

Mailing books and posters back to America turned out to be a time-consuming process. The post office opened every parcel and examined every page of every book we were mailing. We asked what they were looking for and whether there were books that could not be sent, but we received no reply. When we asked if the bookstore wouldn't have known what could and could not be sent, one woman said yes, another said no.

Later we learned through experience that we could not mail any book printed before the Cultural Revolution, no matter how innocuous the subject. Unmailable items were not confiscated, however, and we put several into our suitcases, which were not checked.

Several people have said to us that our positive attitude toward what we saw in China results from the fact that we were shown only positive things and were given preferential treatment. Undoubtedly, there is a grain of truth in this.

CITY LIFE

Voluntary exercising takes place from
5:00 to 7:00 A.M. and is viewed as a pleasant and healthy way to begin the day.
   Chinese physical arts such as shadow
boxing (*Tai Chi Chuan*) and swordplay
are undergoing a revival of interest, in
much the same way as other elements of
ancient Chinese culture—Chinese medicine, for example.

Shanghai

Shanghai

Shanghai

Shanghai

Peking: traffic jam

Shanghai: reading the newspapers

Fushan

Factories generally fall into two categories: handicrafts and other light industries, which often evolved from production by individual artisans to cooperatives and finally to nationalized factories; and heavy industries, which were either nationalized or started after Liberation.

Peking

Fushan

The light industries tend to share the following characteristics, which distinguish them from the heavy industries. Work in the light industries, formerly performed in small individual workshops, requires an apprenticeship. About 50 percent of the workers are women, and the Revolutionary Committees tend to include more women. Workers usually live in nonfactory-associated housing. The factories have nurseries but no day-care centers. Salaries average 50 to 60 yuan per month.

At an ivory carving factory in Canton, almost all the production is for export. Here, as in other factories, workers are assigned to the apprenticeship program on the basis of individual preference balanced by national need.

Artistic ability is not necessarily a criterion, since anyone is believed capable of learning to do any job, with appropriate time and training.

Before Liberation, the apprentice worked for five years and was an indentured servant.

Today, the ivory carving apprenticeship lasts three years, and apprentices receive 22 yuan per month plus a 20 yuan clothing allowance.

When their apprenticeship is completed, workers in this factory are ranked on the basis of skill and seniority (with wages ranging from 40–172 yuan per month), and some people receive 10 extra yuan per month, from a special government fund, because the salary range is low in comparison with other factories in the area. The state council determines the light industry salary scale. In the case of this particular factory, the council offered a subsidy in order to avoid having to restructure the whole light industry wage scale.

The factory was organized in 1955 as a cooperative of 46 members, many of whom had long been ivory carvers or small shop owners. The work schedule is 7:30–11:30 A.M., followed by lunch at home (since most of the workers live close by and "that is the tradition of this factory"), then work again from 1:00–5:00 P.M. There is a fifteen-minute break at 10:00 for exercise, and another at 3:00.

The management of the factory is primarily in the hands of the Revolutionary Committee, its members selected with the approval of higher Party officials. The Revolutionary Committee consists mostly of workers from the factory, since familiarity with the carving process is a necessity for administration. Once a week the cadres participate in the carving work.

The management is divided into several sections. There is a financial section, for accounting; a business section which runs the factory and decides on such matters as the purchase of new machinery; a division devoted to political and labor affairs, to oversee and direct the study sessions in which each worker spends several hours a week; a factory local union; divisions concerned with recreation and literary activities, and with militia training (basically physical education, including ball-playing); and a public-relations division. It is the vice-chairman of this section who greets foreigners and receives guests. There is also a small section called the Section of Creative Design, composed of experienced workers, young workers, and administrative cadres. They create and encourage new designs.

Women retire at 55, and men at 60. Retirees get a lifetime pension, the amount determined by length of service. They may continue to work for as long as they care to. If ill, the worker may retire early.

Maternity leave is 56 paid days after the baby's birth. The factory provides a nursery and allots breast feeding time—half an hour in the morning and in the afternoon, in addition to the usual 15 minute breaks— for as many months as are required.

At all Chinese factories, the work week is six days. All workers get two weeks a year of paid vacation, and eight national holidays: May 1, October 1 (two days), January 1, and Old Chinese New Year, now called Spring Festival (three days). With the authorization of the company doctor, the worker receives full pay for any sick days.

Because the work requires a high degree of skill, the ivory carving factory is unlike many other Chinese factories, in that it does not get students for temporary physical labor.

The Peking Glassware Factory was organized in 1956 from over fifty independent handicraft units. Sixty percent of its workers are women. In some workshops, where glass flowers and animals are made, primarily for export, all of the workers are women. Since the Cultural Revolution they have made buttons as well, to better serve the people.

The Revolutionary Committee consists of seven people: three PLAs, two female cadres, and two workers.

Apprentices are paid 16 yuan per month for the first year, 19 the second, and 22 the third. They also receive 32 yuan a year for clothing.

Other workers get 30–100 yuan; the average is 50, and we found five people making the top salary. The factory offers free showers, haircuts, and movies.

Children under three may attend the nursery, which costs 3–9 yuan per month, depending on the age of the child. The factory pays the nurse and teacher who run it.

The people working in the hot areas receive extra amounts of rationed items such as oil and meat, called nutritional subsidies. Most of these workers are men.

In the Peking Arts and Crafts Factory there are five workshops creating art for export: ivory carving, cloisonné, jade carving, lacquerware, and Chinese traditional painting. Again we were told that no artistic skill is needed to qualify for apprenticeship.

Forty-five percent of the 1,014 employees are women, and there are 50 administrators, of whom 40 percent are women. The pay averages 60 yuan per month. Apprentices get the usual 17, 19, and 22 yuan with 25 yuan per year for clothing, free transportation, and free barbering. Highly skilled veteran workers receive 200 yuan per month. However, there are only three workers who get that much.

The Revolutionary Committee, headed by a woman, is composed of thirteen members: six cadres (two women) and seven workers (two women). The Committee has three sub-committees devoted, respectively, to politics, production, and administration. The political committee has seven members, all of whom are members of the Revolutionary Committee, and it is concerned with political study and attitudes within the factory. The production committee, with fifteen members (two of whom are Revolutionary Committee members), deals with matters of internal finance—salaries, estimating output value, quality control, and equipment. The administrative committee considers worker welfare. Of its five members, one is on the Revolutionary Committee.

There is also a Communist Party committee, which decides who becomes a cadre on the Revolutionary Committee and its subcommittees. The chairman of the Revolutionary Committee is also the Party Committee secretary. The other six members of the Party Committee are selected by the Party members among the factory work force, which in this factory was 10 percent of the workers (15 percent of the young workers are members of the Young Communist League).

Party members select other workers to be members and send the list to the District Party Committee for approval. All workers can express their opinions to the Party members. Three people on the Revolutionary Committee are not Party members.

The heavy industries are larger than the light industries, and the work may require rotating shifts. They offer many more benefits, such as day-care centers and theaters, and provide workers with factory housing. There are fewer women here, and salaries seem to average 60–70 yuan per month. The Revolutionary Committees appear to include more people who are not former workers in the factory, but who are, instead, either PLAs or cadres sent in by the government.

The Wuhan Iron and Steel Works Factory, with its thirty plants and mines, has over 10,000 workers. Despite the fact that the factory is very "labor-intensive," there is much standing around, and the atmosphere is relaxed. Wuhan Iron and Steel has a large day-care center which operates from 7:30 A.M. to 5:00 P.M., during which time the children receive four meals and a bath. Parents pay 8 yuan a month, and the factory pays 7 yuan.

Near the factory-owned workers' housing are a market and a theater. Special food, called health protection food, is cooked for the workers, and sold in the factory cafeteria for very low prices—and this is not counted in the nation-wide rationing system.

Medicine and all medical care are free. If the worker's family lives away from the factory, he is allowed twenty days to go home each year. Retirement age is younger than usual because of the nature of the work—55 for men and 50 for women.

12

There are three work shifts: 8 A.M.–4 P.M., 4 P.M.–12 P.M., and 12 P.M.–8 A.M. Workers rotate so that one week out of three is spent on the night shift. A small minority, including both men and women, work only the day shift, and pregnant or nursing women do not work the night shift.

The average salary is 60 yuan. The highest paid workers get 108 yuan per month, and the highest paid engineers, called technicians, who were engineers before Liberation, get 200 yuan. Those who became engineers after Liberation have salaries more in line with those of the workers. The general policy is gradually to equalize salaries between the worker and the engineer, although some small differentiation will always occur. Only 5 percent of the technicians are women.

The Wuhan Flour Mill, once owned by a Chinese flour magnate, has made several waste-saving innovations since Liberation. The workers are very proud that the wrappers for the noodles they make now come back to the factory for reuse, and that the leftover skin, beard, and ashes of the wheat now are made into medicine for scabies. Twelve full-time workers are in charge of this process. The workers were also responsible for the creation and building of a new semi-automatic packaging system.

Besides sick leave (5 percent of the work force asks for sick leave each year), the worker can also take leave for personal business. If he wants one day off, he sees his immediate superior, for two, he sees that man's superior, and for three or more, he must see the highest manager. The frequency of asking for leave depends on the individual worker's "self-realization"—his perception of his place in the scheme of the Revolution. There are five circumstances warranting leaves: sickness, private business, seeing relatives, funerals, for which three days are alloted for the funeral of anyone lineally related (parents and children, but not brothers or sisters), and weddings (one's own or that of a close relative) for which the worker is allowed three days, or one month including travel should his future spouse live far away.

Peking: counting the payroll

At the Shenyang Transformer Factory transformers and testers are made for high-tension wires. Before Liberation there were 200 workers. Today there are 5,050.

From 1950–53 and 1958–60, this factory was helped by Russian technicians. The factory acknowledged to us its gratitude to Stalin for all past Soviet assistance.

Like others, this self-supporting factory processes all its own materials, even making its own insulators. Transport needs are minimized, and in case of war factories not under attack can continue to function.

This factory suffered only one month of interruption during the Cultural Revolution. Two sides were attacking the factory leadership on various grounds, but there was little work stoppage, although from time to time the workers came out of their shops to see what was happening, we were told.

Since the Cultural Revolution, regular study sessions have a new critical importance. The Shenyang workers have political study on Tuesday and Saturday afternoons from 3–5. The workers study in small groups, and the cadres study together. On Thursday afternoons from 4–6, there is cultural or technical study. One hour is work time, the other is the individual's own time. Technical experts use this session to teach the workers how to improve their performance. The cultural study is primarily for old workers without much schooling—during this time they may learn to read and write.

The leaders who were attacked during the Cultural Revolution are still working at this factory. Before the Cultural Revolution they had an eight-person leadership, of whom five are still leaders. The chairman of the Political section before the Cultural Revolution was raised to chairman of the Revolutionary Committee. The original chairman of the Revolutionary Committee was raised to manager of all electric factories in the Tientsin municipal government.

Before the Cultural Revolution more weight was given to technical qualifications; now the individual's political viewpoint is more important. However, two engineers are on the present Revolutionary Committee. The current membership of the Revolutionary Committee includes twenty-eight people: four PLAs drawn from among those PLAs who came to the factory as part of government propaganda teams during the Cultural Revolution, eight cadres, and sixteen workers. The present term of office is indeterminate, since the whole system is in a state of reorganization. There are five criteria for this office: the candidate must be an assiduous student of Chairman Mao's thoughts; he must be devoted to serving the people; he must be brave in criticism, and brave in self-criticism; he must be intimately linked with the masses; and he must have established solidarity with the cadres, with the masses, and with those who have criticized him.

Each section of the factory nominates twenty-eight people, not necessarily from their own section. These names are then posted, and each worker votes for twenty-eight. If too many names still remain, they vote again.

The cadres we spoke with admitted that it is unrealistic to say that all people in China put the public good before self. But they claim that the best way to reform people is to instruct them in Chairman Mao's thoughts, teach them to struggle against selfishness and criticize revisionism, to be self-critical, and to hold up models—individuals who are exemplaries. And, they add, "our socialist system encourages this."

Workers in the heavy industries appeared to be under less pressure than those in light industry, who all seemed to be working intently at their desks.

Whether in light or heavy industry, the factory worker, along with the farmer and the soldier, is part of the elite of the new Chinese society, and his daily life illustrates clearly the socialist ideal toward which China is struggling.

Fushan

Peking: Great Wall Peach Cannery

Sian: textile mill

At the Tientsin #1 Rug Factory the cafeteria offers lunches for 15 fen with no meat,
and 25 fen with meat. The worker may
bring his own lunch, and facilities are available if he wishes to cook it at the factory.

Sian: textile mill

Peking: heavy machinery factory

Peking: heavy machinery factory

Peking: heavy machinery factory

Shanghai

From time to time the entire factory listens to the loudspeaker. Every day at 11:30 A.M. (lunchtime) there is a broadcast, which might be an announcement, or someone relating an experience, or some selections from Chairman Mao's thoughts. A current favorite slogan is: "Standing beside the machine, your ancestral land in your bosom, but your eyes on the rest of the world."

Peking: heavy machinery factory

Peking: heavy machinery factory

Shanghai

Peking

Peking

Every working day during the hot summer months people take after-lunch naps.

Peking: glass-factory nursery

Sian: textile mill

The Peking Embroidery and Appliqué Factory has 700 workers, over 85 percent of whom are women. In addition, 8,000 housewives work at home. Again, most items—tablecloths, curtains, pillowcases, etc.—are for export.

Salaries average only 40 yuan per month, with a high of 80 and a low of 30. Housewives working at home are paid by the piece, and they average 30 yuan per month.

This Revolutionary Committee, with seven members, includes six women and is headed by a woman.

Most workers live outside the factory, although a few single men live in factory dormitories. Single women live at home. There is no dining room. Workers bring their own meals, and the factory steams them.

Until they are three-and-a-half, children may attend the factory nursery. Then, since there is no day-care center, they must go to another district kindergarten at a cost of 12–13 yuan per month.

Peking: a tapestry of the Great Wall being completed at an embroidery and appliqué factory

Cases of industrial accidents are handled in the following ways. When a worker is injured he gets sick leave with pay, and all expenses are taken care of. For a deformity which does not prevent working, the worker is reassigned with his original salary. If totally disabled he receives 60 percent of his original salary, more if he has worked many years. If he has worked twenty-five years, the worker gets 100 percent of salary.

Should a worker be killed, his children are taken care of until the age of 16 to 18, whenever they finish middle school and go to work. If a wife does not work, the factory will care for her until she finds a job. She also gets a small amount of compensation, depending on the deceased's monthly salary. I could not find out whether a man receives compensation for his wife's death.

Peking: Great Wall Peach Cannery

Peking

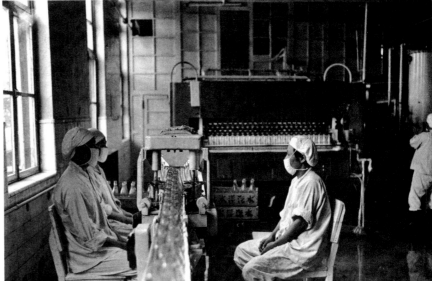

Peking: inspecting soda bottles

25

Peking

At the Peking #2 Cotton Textile Mill there is factory housing that covers over 200,000 square meters. We visited the housing and met one family.

Ch'u Ah-ling, age 55, was originally from Shanghai. She used to work in this mill and is now retired with a 60 percent pension. Her husband, Ku P'ei-ken, 59, works in this mill and, as an old worker, gets 102 yuan. Their son, 38, works in a nearby machine tool factory, and his wife, 35, works at this textile mill. The two grandsons, aged 12 and 9, are in school. All of them and a 16-year-old daughter, also in school, live in one apartment, for which they pay 6.80 yuan per month (including electricity and water). Gas is .50 yuan per month per person, but if there are more than seven people in a household, the cost is only .25 each. The entire household has a combined monthly salary of 240 yuan, of which more than 100 is spent on food. This figure was much higher than other figures we had heard, but we learned that this family lives quite luxuriously because they have four salaries. There are three other daughters who are no longer at home: one, aged 35, is with the Shanghai telephone bureau, another, 27, is a doctor in Wuhan, and the third, 22, is a farmer in Yenan.

The Northwest State-Owned #4 Cotton Textile Mill in Sian includes a sports ground, pool, library, clinics and medical centers, nurseries, and a primary and middle school with 4,800 students. There are fifteen buildings of apartments, housing 1,520 families, and six buildings for singles, housing 2,500 people.

The first home we visited contained three rooms for eight people—two grandparents (the grandfather retired from this mill with a pension of 80 yuan, from a salary of 103.50), a son and his wife, two daughters, and two grandsons. Another son is in the army. For these three rooms with private bath and kitchen they pay 6 yuan. The combined family income is over 200 yuan. The grandmother stays home and does the housework. Sometimes the family eats in the factory, at a cost of approximately 15 yuan per month per person. To eat at home costs approximately 10 yuan per month per person.

Another family, the Tungs, consists of seven members, of whom four live together in two rooms. The father works as a machinery repairman and earns 87 yuan. The mother, now retired from loom work, receives a 40 yuan pension from a salary of 60 yuan. A 21-year-old son works in this mill and earns 32 yuan. A daughter, 16, is in school. Altogether, they spend 4 yuan on rent. On their rest days they go to the park, the movies, or the club for workers which this factory sponsors. Every Saturday evening workers or theater groups perform. There is some kind of show almost every night, and it is easy for factory workers to get tickets.

Last year on Mr. Tung's vacation the couple visited Mr. Tung's younger brother and sister in Dairen. Generally, they see their relatives once or twice a year, and sometimes relatives visit them. The children see the relatives perhaps once in three years. Their eldest son, who is a car driver in Sian, comes over frequently, and their daughter, who works in the #5 mill, lives nearby and also visits often.

Mr. Liu, a member of our reception committee, is secretary of the Revolutionary Committee, a position he has held for two years. He began as a worker at this mill in 1956, and in 1966 he became a cadre-administrator. At 35 he earns 65 yuan. In 1960, he married a girl he had known since primary school. He lives in one of the bachelor apartments at this mill, for which he pays .70 yuan, while his wife, who works in another part of Sian, lives in single-person housing there. Their two children, aged 11 and 7, live on a commune in the nearby countryside with their grandparents. Every Sunday, his rest day, Mr. Liu goes to see the children. Mrs. Liu also visits the children on her rest day, which is not Sunday, so the parents rarely see one another.

A female office worker on the reception committee has been working at this mill since 1956 and is trying to become a Party member. Her three children, aged 17, 15, and 12, live at home with her and her husband, a driver who earns 70 yuan. Her salary is 65 yuan, and they pay 2 yuan for a one-room apartment. The eldest son works in a steel mill in Sian.

The third member of our reception committee was also a woman. For fifteen years she has been a designer, and now, at 38, she earns 47 yuan. She is also trying to become a Party member. Her husband, 39, works at a machine factory as a technician, and earns 82 yuan. Both are college graduates. With their 9-year-old child they live in a one-room apartment belonging to the husband's factory, for which they pay 2 yuan. They share a kitchen with another family.

Peking

We spent one evening in Shanghai with three former industrialists. One had spent two years in Milwaukee with Ellis-Chalmers, one had graduated from Trinity College, Cambridge, and the third had gone to Harvard. All came from immensely wealthy families. In fact, the father of one had been kidnapped twice by corrupt officials in pre-Liberation days. The first time the ransom requested and received was $500,000. The second time, the family had no difficulty in fulfilling the demand for $1 million.

The gist of our conversation that evening follows.

Thanks partly to American imperialism, which manifested itself in the form of exports to China of such goods as cotton which the Chinese government did not have the power to limit, inflation was rampant in pre-Liberation days. In 1937, 100 Chinese dollars bought two oxen, but in 1947, the same amount bought one charcoal briquette. In 1949, 100 Chinese dollars could not purchase one grain of rice. The workers suffered the most because they had fixed wages.

Mr. L. found himself continuously undersold by the United States, so he had to close his cement factory, forcing the workers to leave the premises at bayonet-point. Some were beaten to death; others were sent to jail for one to ten years. Mr. L. turned his factory into a warehouse to store American cement. "Not until the Cultural Revolution did I see to such an intense extent how cruel we were," he said.

Another industrialist, Mr. Y., had two brothers who went to Brazil when it seemed that the Communists were going to win. He and his father did not want to leave their factories, so they stayed. In those days there were many rumors circulating about the Communists and their hatred of capitalists. Some of the rumors claimed that the industrialists would either be buried alive or sent to hard labor in Siberia.

The PLA marched into Shanghai, and Mr. Y. was impressed with their discipline, courtesy, and friendliness: "Even in the rain they didn't go into people's houses." Mr. Y. and his father received an invitation from Chen Yi, the mayor of Shanghai (and 27 later foreign minister of China), and the Military Control Commission to come in for talks. They selected for the occasion their worst clothes. Mr. Y. wore his old student garb and had his driver stop the car far away so he could walk to the meeting. The officials told him that they wanted to achieve solidarity with the national capitalists, but not with the bureaucratic capitalists who worked in conjunction with American imperialists, which pleased Mr. Y. The Communists told him to get going and open up his factories.

It took a year for the industrialists to feel certain of the situation with the Communists. They were all impressed with the honesty of the leaders and cadres. Mr. L. got into trouble for trying to bribe the Communists: he couldn't believe that a government official could not be bought. They were also amazed to find that, in six months, the Communists had stabilized prices. "I studied economics at Cambridge," Mr. L. said, "but I couldn't find it in my textbooks how to do that."

"In the beginning we still tried to make

Peking

money, speculating, hedging, hoarding. We thought no one could put Shanghai in order. In six months the prostitutes, the crime and corruption disappeared.

"The Cultural Revolution was tough for us. We were mentally unprepared. We were afraid that the Communists were going to get rid of us. This movement aroused our workers. We capitalists feared mass struggle most of all. Mr. Y. and I were told to do manual labor in the factory. Why should I, a well-educated, British-educated person do manual labor?

"We are still doing it: Mr. Y. does it all the time, I do it three times a week, eight hours a day. We also study, both by ourselves and with other capitalists.

"Liu Shao-c'hi said, 'Let the capitalists manage—they are good managers.' But these six years [since the Cultural Revolution] have been the most valuable years of my life. I never had a chance to get to know the workers. I used to think that I created wealth by my smartness. Now I know that wealth is not easy to create—you need sweat and brains. I thought the workers

would be tough with me, and they were. They told me that they had a responsibility to me, to help my thoughts as well as my work.

"The workers were smart—I saw that they knew how to do things, how to solve problems that would come up on the job. I could see that the workers were very responsible. If something went wrong in the factory they felt the hurt, as if it were their own property. I didn't. So I apologized to them, but they said, 'Don't apologize to us; we are all serving the people.'

"More and more I feel closer to the workers. Recalling the past is a powerful ideological weapon. You feel how closely your fate is tied up with the socialist cause. You hear a whole hall of people weeping because they all lost some dear ones."

Shanghai

The prices of food vary slightly from area to area and are determined by the planning committee of the provincial government. For example, before the cucumber season each local committee decides the number of cucumbers that will be needed for the local population. Cucumbers are available only in season. However, if there is a cucumber failure, the committee will try to have an adequate supply of cucumbers imported from another province, such as Kwangtung, where the growing season is longer. These imported cucumbers will sell at the original price, even at the risk of a financial loss.

Canton: commune

Peking

A small amount of private enterprise is allowed. The Chinese government differentiates between property necessary for existence and property sufficient to yield a profit. The former is private; the latter is national. Street hawkers of popsicles, for example, operate privately. These may be old people whose 12 yuan old-age pension (available to anyone with no other source of income) is not adequate, and who do not have relatives willing or able to assist them. If the Revolutionary Street Committee of the neighborhood decides that an individual needs an additional source of income, then they allow him to set up a business of this type.

Canton: commune store

Peking

Peking

Shanghai: man purchasing a hearing aid for his mother in a medical supply house

Shanghai

Shanghai

Peking

Despite China's size and huge population, information can be swiftly transmitted. Besides the *People's Daily* (*Jen-min Jih-pao*), an official newspaper for public consumption, each work unit publishes a newspaper, exclusively for its members, which contains both world and local news.

Personal information also may be readily conveyed. Leaving China, Dick and I made a brief stop at the Wuhan airport, several miles from the city. Later we learned that someone had told my uncle in Wuhan that we had been at the airport. My uncle, an ordinary worker, knows no one who works at the airport, but the connection was made because somebody remembered my face.

Another time, one of our group unknowingly dropped two Hong Kong coins in the dirt at Choukoutien, many miles outside of Peking. Two days later, on our visit to the Institute for Vertebrate Paleontology and Paleoanthropology in Peking, the cadre who received us pulled the coins out of his breast pocket and returned them.

Shanghai

Shanghai

CITYSCAPE

Pataling: the Great Wall

Shanghai

Yenan: the Revolutionary Museum and a portrait of Chairman Mao as a young man

Peking: entrance to the Forbidden City. Tourists from all over China flock to this spot.

Sian: the hot springs

Shanghai

Since every work unit has a different rest day, the public parks are filled with people every day of the week. During the Cultural Revolution, card-playing was frowned on, so people still do not like to have their pictures taken at the card table. These boys are about to leap up and disappear.

Shanghai

Shanghai

Shanghai

While there is little public display of affection in China, the couples one sees in any park, restaurant, or street, walking, sitting, or riding bicycles together, are courting.

For a Chinese couple to spend time alone together is an admission of romantic intent. Occasionally, in the dim light of evening, a few couples can be seen holding hands, especially in Shanghai which has long been known as a "fast" city. Such a casual scene as a young man taking a photograph of a young woman is full of meaning, and I was told by one man that he knew his wife was truly serious about him when, during their courtship, she finally allowed him to take her picture.

At the time of our visit, we knew of a romance between a 24-year-old woman named A and a 26-year-old man from Szechwan named S, a PLA cadre in a school and Young Communist League member, who was then stationed in central China. Far away from his own parents, he requested the assistance of a friend's mother in finding him a mate, and she suggested A, the daughter of one of her friends. He was interested, and the woman described S to A's mother. S by this time had peeked at A secretly on her way home from work.

S then wrote several long letters to A's father describing himself and his background. S stated his intentions—marriage. He also sent his diary and his photo album.

A's father answered none of the letters. Then, one day he told A about S and said he was going to invite him to visit the family as an ordinary guest. A said nothing. Her mother and her matchmaker friend had many long talks about S.

S and his friend's mother visited unexpectedly when A and her mother were out. S brought cakes, red wine, and a few other gifts, which were all accepted. He was offered tea, and some small talk ensued. Since S's family is from Szechwan, and so is A's mother's family, it was suggested that the families might be related. A finally came home from work, but she did not speak to S.

S then visited three more times.

S has written A many letters which she neither answers nor discusses with her family. She still does not talk to S when he visits. 49

Although her father likes S and says he is honest, trustworthy, open, and generous, A insists she will never marry but wants to take care of her family and continue the revolution. S still visits and assists A's family: when they went on a trip he took them to the boat and picked them up on their return. What happens next depends entirely on A. S is not deterred by A's manifestations of disinterest. S and A are having a fairly traditional Chinese courtship.

In today's China, however, women can now approach men through a third party. Then one may ask the other for tea or a meal, or the man may buy lunch for the woman. Sometimes the woman may be invited to the man's house after work.

It is quite acceptable to end the venture after a few cups of tea. It is also acceptable to "break up" after a long time, but then the two parties are expected to discuss the situation.

Love letters are still written. The act of writing the letter is as full of meaning as the content. While some couples hold hands or kiss, my own cousins tell me that they never touched before marriage.

Courtship may continue for several years. The government encourages late marriage —the guideline is 26 for women, 28 for men. To marry, you simply fill out a license and have witnesses sign it. Some people hold a small party with a few close friends or relatives.

To obtain a divorce (which is still fairly rare), one must first go through a period of discussion about the problems in the marriage with the head of each party's work unit, the heads of the Revolutionary Street Committee, and so on. If, after several months of intense discussion, the couple still want the divorce, it is granted.

We were told in Shanghai that during the Cultural Revolution some people wanted divorces from politically contaminated partners, but that some of these couples have since reconciled.

Shanghai

Shanghai

Every worker, farmer, and soldier in China attends regular study sessions (*hsueh hsi*) several times a week with a small group of fellow workers. Although some of these sessions are "technical" (to improve skills, such as reading) or "business" (administrative) meetings, the most important and frequent are "political" sessions.

The political study sessions concentrate on the application of theory to daily life. While self-criticism or criticism of fellow workers is an integral part of these sessions, this does not necessarily cause them to take on hostile or humiliating overtones. The point of the exercise is for everyone present to learn.

When theory is the focus of discussion, it is always applied to the worker's own context. During our visit to the Institute for Vertebrate Paleontology and Paleoanthropology, study sessions were focussed on the Paris Commune of the French Revolution. Participants were reading Marx's essays in *The Civil War in France,* with an

introduction by Engels, and discussing how the conclusions did and did not apply to China. The effort was intended to point out to the workers the influence of historical context on political activity.

We asked their view of the United States' system of government in the light of Marxism-Leninism. First there was silence, then the leading cadre present answered:

"Power is in the hands of the big capitalists, and there is no difference between Democrats and Republicans. Internal revolution is inevitable, because there is oppression both outside the United States and inside. However, we agree that at present the conflict in America is not sharp enough, because Americans can go outside their country to oppress others, but, as the Afro-Asian countries stand on their own, the capitalists will only be able to oppress those in their own country, so the internal conflict will precipitate revolution. Fundamentally, the production system and resource control of America determine the political

Peking: park outside the Temple of Heaven

system and create internal contradictions which cannot be solved."

When we asked why it is that in the United States the workers and proletariat are the most right-wing, anti-Communist class, and the upper-middle-class intellectuals and students the most left-wing, he replied:

"We differentiate between revolutionary potential and revolutionary actuality. Among poor farmers, the potential is greater than among intellectuals, but, because of poor education in these matters, they have no way of understanding their potential. We have cases here of poor farmers who were given land and secretly returned it to the rich landlord because they didn't realize the significance of their act.

"The important word is *chueh-wu*—realization. Realization is not possible without the leadership of the Communist Party. We are allowing for a long historical process in the United States. There may be an interim group, à la the North Vietnamese Labor Party, but the end result will be Communism."

Chengchou: pictures of Marx, Engels, Lenin, and Stalin in a public pagoda

Peking: PLAs in front of the Forbidden City

53

Near Pataling

Yenan: the Revolutionary Museum

54

My father asked a taxi driver in Peking to take him to a church, and found himself at a mosque. There are still many thousands of Moslems in China, and, particularly in the Peking area, it is not difficult to find a Moslem restaurant. Although other Chinese are encouraged to cremate their dead, the Moslems, who object to cremation, are still allowed burial.

Other religions, however, do not seem to have flourished. We visited a lamasery in Peking and were greeted by several members of the Revolutionary Committee and by a shy little lama wearing a blue Mao cap, a patched white jacket, blue pants, and black shoes. We were led to a beautiful reception room, furnished with old rugs, hangings, and vases, but with new teacups.

We were told that this temple used to derive most of its revenue from funerals and from the rental of houses and land. Since Liberation, the state has given it over one million yuan for refurbishing. There are still twenty-five lamas who live here and take care of the fruit trees (as their physical labor), selling the products for income. They read scriptures, and, like everyone else, study the works of Chairman Mao. There are some worshipers—Mongols, Tibetans, some Chinese, and a few Manchus—who come to the temple on their rest days, but in general the temple is undisturbed. It was one of the few totally quiet and serene places we visited in China. The thousands of scriptures stacked along the walls, each wrapped in many layers of cloth, were heavily laden with dust, and had obviously not been read for a long time. There was some rebuilding going on and the government appears to be keeping the temple in readiness.

The South Church of Peking, a Catholic Church, functions on a limited level. At Sunday mass we noticed that the worshippers were all foreigners—diplomats and tourists, except for one wizened Chinese lady.

The grounds outside looked neglected. There was no grass or flowers, and the front gate was closed. Inside all was in good repair, although there were no prayer books, and lights instead of candles.

The Chinese bishop and his assistant, Father Tien, conducted the ceremony in almost inaudible Chinese. There was no music and no feeling of congregation. A few of the worshippers brought their own prayer books. Later, the old Chinese lady and a middle-aged Chinese woman took communion with the foreigners. The service ended as anti-climatically as it had begun, as the bishop and the priest disappeared and the lights went off.

The bishop and his assistant came back into the church in Mao suits, where a large white man and his son were waiting for them. The bishop seemed to know them well. The two men talked, then the son talked to the bishop. Finally, the father bent to kiss the bishop's ring and walked away. It was the first time I had seen foreigners and Chinese interacting in China so intimately.

We went to the reception room to talk with Father Tien. Again, as at the temple, the room was furnished with many old screens, chairs, and vases, and there were good rugs on the floor. With no explanation, the cadre from the lamasery was present. We later guessed that, because religion is relatively inactive at this time, one cadre, from the State Council Commission on Religion, is in charge of all the institutions in each area.

Shanghai

Peking: inside the Forbidden City

Shanghai

Peking: The calligraphy is in Chairman Mao's handwriting.

Peking: All-Peking Junior and Senior Middle School Swim Meet

We went to both large international sports contests in huge modern stadiums and small local ones in little outdoor amphitheaters. Genuine sportsmanship was displayed on the field as well as in the stands. Audiences impartially applauded every good point, and there was absolutely no booing. Tea and towels were periodically served to each team by members of the other team. Several times we noticed that excessively rough playing on the part of a foreign team was not reciprocated by the Chinese team. The players were there, as they announced at the beginning of each game, to learn from one another, and not to compete violently.

Peking: the judge's stand

Peking: Prizes include plaques and books or pencil boxes.

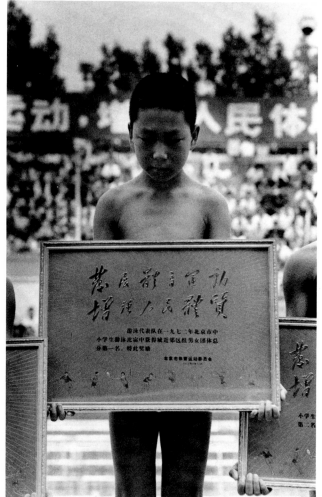

Occasionally we saw scalpers outside big events surrounded by anxious crowds waving 10-fen notes. Inside, there was constant movement in the aisles and talking in the crowd. Once, two girls who wanted to sit together asked the man in front of us whether he would change tickets. When he replied negatively, they both sat, one in front of the other, in the same seat.

The loudspeaker frequently made announcements: "Comrade X, your child is waiting for you outside." "So and so, who works for Ching Hua Printing Company,

your family has urgent business—please go home." "Little friend X from Y school, your older brother is waiting for you on the south side." "Driver of such and such a small car, please move it. You are blocking the way."

At a small volleyball game between the Sian and Tientsin girls' teams the announcer kept up a steady conversation throughout the evening. "Tientsin always finds a way, no matter how difficult the ball," after a good shot, and, "The players show concern for each other by serving the opposite team drinks and towels in each time out." He also made jokes: "The score this time was 15–8, last time it was 8–15. It's as though they have exchanged scores." When the announcer commented that a player admitted having touched the net, although the official had not noticed it, the crowd applauded. The only time the announcer lost his hold over the audience was when he asked them to remain in the stadium until after the foreign guests had left. There was a minor stampede for the exits.

Peking: Most of the spectators are workers on their rest days and children on summer vacation.

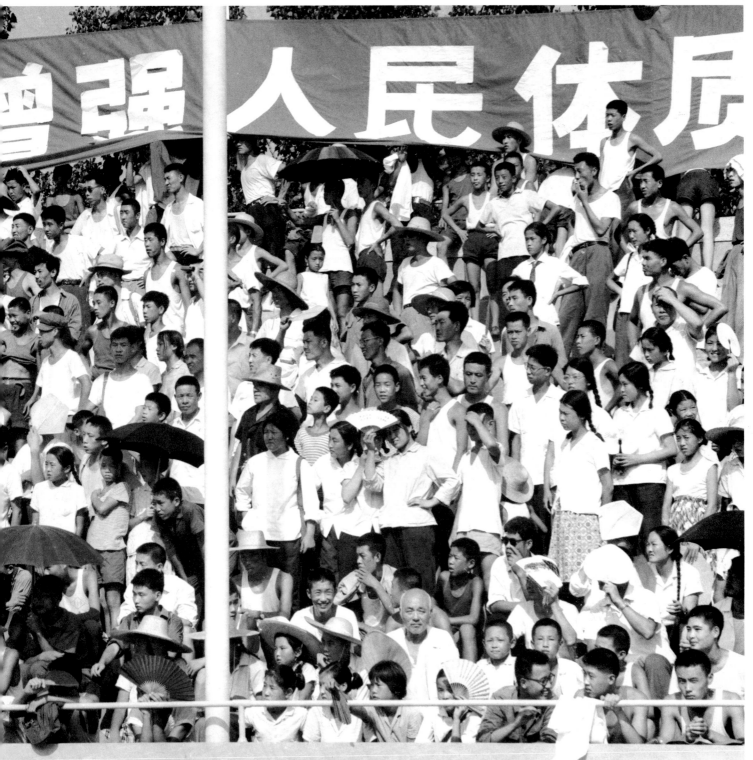

Education at all levels is still in a state of flux. During the Cultural Revolution most schools were closed. Students, teachers, administrators, textbooks, and the entire educational process underwent extensive reevaluation and reorganization. During our visit the Chinese were experimenting with the schools in efforts to shorten the educational process by cutting out the unnecessary (thus producing more educated people within the limits of the available resources), and to base the educational process on reality—on the needs of the workers, peasants, and soldiers. The educated person is expected to use his skills to better the lot of all Chinese, to serve the people. The equality of physical and intellectual labor is stressed to students and teachers. All students and teachers must participate in regularly scheduled physical labor. Study sessions and course material stress the importance of combining practical knowledge with experience. The aim of the primary and secondary school system in China today is to turn out a cultured worker with a social conscience.

We visited three middle schools: the Wuhan #4 Middle School, where my grandmother used to teach in the primary division and where she and my mother once lived; the 23rd Middle School of Wuhan, where my mother went to high school; and the former Nankai Middle School in Tientsin, from which my father was expelled for playing Chinese operatic arias (which were thought to be immoral) on a musical instrument in the dormitory and failing four subjects. For a finale, he had eaten so frequently at the food shops opposite the school that he had to pawn his luggage in order to get home.

All of these schools were formerly boarding schools, two exclusively for boys, and the third for girls. Now they are all coeducational, neighborhood schools. In education, as in all else, the government is trying to eliminate vast geographical differences in standards.

Shanghai: performance at the Children's Palace. The red neckerchiefs indicate that they are Little Red Soldiers.

Canton: day care center. The winners of the tug-of-war spontaneously shouted, "Long Live Chairman Mao," very excitedly.

Shanghai: a children's palace. These girls gave a demonstration in which they shot down plastic airplanes attached to balloons.

Since the Cultural Revolution, educational institutions have made a special effort to appoint former workers as administrators. In many cases these workers have not themselves completed primary school, but they are expected to provide proper moral (political) guidance. Their experience with physical labor enables them to counterbalance the tendency of intellectuals to denigrate the importance of physical labor, and thus ignore its lessons.

For this reason, the official school year, which runs from the middle of February to the middle of July, and then from the end of August to the end of December, includes two months (one each semester) of physical labor in the fields or factories. The entire class goes as a unit with the teacher. In addition, each of the schools we visited included at least one factory where students make such things as transistors. These factories are not frivolous; the items produced are sold; machinery consists primarily of recycled castoffs from larger factories which the students have repaired. The idea is for the students to learn the spirit

as much as the method of working, and so there are several veteran workers who teach in these school factories.

The Tientsin school, for example, has a workshop where desks, beds, and chairs are made, for which the government pays the school. There are three veteran workers in the shop. The school hopes to be economically semi-independent in ten to fifteen years, but that is not the purpose of the program. The work is viewed as a learning process whereby students must test their theories against reality. The schools also have fields where they grow crops. At the school where my grandmother used to teach there is a cotton field where the tennis courts once were.

There are nine years of compulsory education in the city and in those communes with a superior economy. Poorer communes have seven years. Primary school has been experimentally compressed into five years, and secondary or middle school has been shortened from five to four years, divided into lower and upper middle school.

The class schedule at one school was as follows: Students arrive at school for physical exercise (summer only) at 7:00 A.M. From 7:20–7:50 A.M., they do homework, and from 8:00–11:45 A.M., they attend classes in 4 forty-five-minute periods. Students go home for lunch from 11:35 A.M.– 2:30 P.M. (In winter, lunch ends at 2:00, so afternoon classes are over earlier). From 2:30–4:20 P.M., there are more classes, and after that time, there are extracurricular activities as well as some laboratories.

Students pay 4 yuan per term for electricity, water, etc., but they need not pay if they are unable. Any child who needs it may request 6 yuan per term for expenses, in case, for example, a child has to support his parents. In the Tientsin school, 180 of the 4,800 students were receiving school aid.

Middle-school subjects are as follows: In the first year of middle school, students study politics, Chinese language, mathematics (with an emphasis on solving industrial problems), history, geography, foreign language (assigned, not chosen— current assignments include English, Japanese and Russian), music, art, and ath-

letics. The second year consists of politics, Chinese, mathematics, physics, a foreign language, biology (called foundations of agriculture), history, music, art, and athletics. The third and fourth year curricula are the same, and they include politics, Chinese, mathematics, physics, chemistry, a foreign language, and athletics.

Grading is on a 100 point system, and 60 percent is passing. Almost no one repeats a year or drops out, because his parents, teachers, and classmates will all help him keep up. Students are not in competition with each other.

Each semester a *chien-ting* is held, in which each pupil criticizes the character and work of others. First, each student (and teacher) writes a self-estimation of his performance during the semester. Then others read it aloud and discuss it. Both pupils and teacher participate, and the composite report is filed as part of the student's dossier. The emphasis is on constructive criticism—"positive education."

Should a teacher need help with his teaching, several teachers may collectively prepare for classes. Each week, there is at least one night time teachers' study group. In Wuhan there is a once-a-week meeting for all Wuhan teachers in each discipline, offering teachers continuous education in their particular area. These meetings may involve an outside lecturer from a university, or else a visit to a research facility, and discussion of what was learned. Some disciplines may meet only every other week.

Salaries are distributed on two scales, one for teachers and one for administrators. The teachers' salary scale runs from 1 to 10 (like a civil-service ranking) with 1 being the highest. Only two teachers out of seventy-four in the Nankai Middle School receive grade 1 salaries: 149.50 yuan per month. The majority are ranked around 4 (89.50 yuan), 5 (75.50 yuan), and 6 (70 yuan). Administrators' salaries are ranked on a scale from 1 to 24, but no one in China has grade 1 (500 yuan). We were told that Chairman Mao and Premier Chou had voluntarily lowered their ranks to grade 3. No one we met knew of a school principal who ranked above grade 13.

Shanghai: a children's palace. The soldier is teaching Morse code. The sentence on the board is "Long Live Chairman Mao." Chinese characters are transmitted by number, then translated back into characters at point of receipt.

65

The lowest ranked administrators and teachers are those who have just begun to work. After one year they are automatically raised one grade, but then raises come more slowly. They are granted on the basis of years of service, the evaluations of colleagues, and the consent of the leadership. The teacher or administrator is judged on morality (politics) and ability. However, the total number of teachers that can be raised to the next grade is nationally determined by the state of the economy. Therefore, if there are no vacancies in one grade, there is no purpose in raising someone to it. In recent years raises have occurred in 1951, 1953, 1956, 1960, 1963. In 1972 the

Shanghai

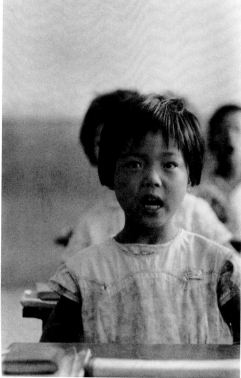

Shanghai

Shanghai: city commune. A formal recitation for visitors.

raises were not for the whole sum, but a partial raise did take place.

School employees, like other Chinese workers, have a non-obligatory retirement age of 55 for women and 60 for men. The pension they receive depends on length of work and ranges from 60 to 100 percent of previous salary.

Although there is no PTA, the teacher visits the students' homes frequently. In Wuhan, my cousin's teacher came over to meet us, and she seemed very close to my cousin and her family. Once or twice a semester there may be a parents' meeting in the school.

When we asked about juvenile delinquency we were told that there are a few juvenile delinquents, whom the school attempts to reeducate. If the child is a repeater, he may be sent to a labor camp, which is like a reform school for young people only. It was claimed that the most common types of delinquents are those who have been influenced by capitalistic thoughts and thus are led to steal or pick pockets. There is also occasional truancy, in which case the teacher will seek the cooperation of the child's family.

There are rewards for especially outstanding children, in the form of membership in a special honor group. In primary school, that group is known as the Little

Peking

Red Soldiers (*hung hsiao ping*), recognizable by their red neckerchiefs, which they wear at all times. These children are chosen by their fellow classmates as well as their teachers, and they must not only demonstrate scholastic, artistic, or athletic ability, but also correct attitudes (politics) toward others. By the end of primary school, almost every child is expected to become a Little Red Soldier.

In secondary school, however, it becomes quite difficult again to attain this special honor, which is now called the Red Guard (*hung wei ping*). Very few junior and senior middle school pupils eventually become Red Guards. Depending on the geographic area, they can be identified by either a red badge or a red armband, again worn at all times. (Although the name is the same, this is not the Red Guard of the Cultural Revolution. College students are no longer Red Guards, although some of them are former Red Guards from the Cultural Revolution.) These new Red Guards are expected to set a good example for the other children, and they are quite conscious of their special status. Their chances of being accepted in a high status position in the future, such as PLA, cadre, or college student, are greatly enhanced.

A 13-year-old boy, who is a neighbor of my grandmother's, showed me an English spelling flash-card book he had made. Each page held one word, with indications of pronunciation. Some of the words were: village, pigsty, freedom, hatred, reeducation, discussion, proletarian, home, battalion, dedicate, wholly, actively, interest, goodness, beautiful, city, whole, remember, mean, life-blood, ideological, correctness, decide, everything, dependent, out, wait, return, sweep, yard, carry, water, example, accept, back, yesterday, farm-work, profound, pupil, criticize, just, statement.

Peking

Preventing the formation of elites—one of the major social contradictions of Chinese communism, and the problem often cited as the cause of the Cultural Revolution—has reshaped almost every aspect of university life. All the universities we visited had been closed for several years following the Cultural Revolution, and were not yet back in full operation. They had enrolled, at the time of our visit, only one or two classes numbering at most one-third of previous capacity. The aim of current educational experiments is to prevent the creation of a technical elite divorced from the masses, from productive labor, and from reality. The professional staff in charge of the administration before the Cultural Revolution has been replaced by a political staff. This change has not meant a complete change in personnel. But, although the numbers may vary, the balance of the Revolutionary Committee is always heavily weighted toward members with political rather than technical expertise.

At Tsinghua the committee consists of six faculty members, six workers and technicians, five cadres, five students, four PLAs, one family dependent and four members from a Chairman Mao Propaganda unit.

At Liaoning University the pre-Cultural Revolution administration included one president, who was also Party secretary, three vice-presidents and three vice-secretaries. The president died of illness in 1966. One former vice-president was investigated and cleared, and is now back on the current Revolutionary Committee. Another vice-president is still being investigated, which means that the authorities are reviewing the history of his work, his utterances and his behavior. Meanwhile he works at the university reshaping texts. The third former vice-president is too old to work but he has been cleared.

Two of the former vice-secretaries are back on the present Revolutionary Committee. The third is being disciplined. He and his family have moved, and he now works in a mine.

There is no board of trustees. Outsiders involved with the university, such as the PLAs on the Revolutionary Committee, are involved full-time.

The Revolutionary Committee is the administration of the college; its chairman is equivalent to the college president. He is usually a national Party member cadre, appointed by the Party.

Each academic department also has a Revolutionary Committee, composed solely of department members, unless the department's political strength is considered weak (in which case outside leadership may be sent in). The chairman of the department is chairman of the departmental Revolutionary Committee.

On a higher level, the university is under dual control. Politically, it is controlled by the cadres appointed by the Party Central Committee. Educationally, it is controlled by the Scientific and Education Group of the State Council, with Premier Chou En-lai its chairman. As a result, the curricula and administration of all Chinese universities is fairly uniform, reflecting government efforts to standardize the quality of education.

Each province now has only one comprehensive university, offering both arts and sciences, which accepts only local applicants. In many cases the comprehensive university was formerly the most elite university in the province. All other universities have become polytechnical or teacher training colleges. A few provinces, such as Tibet, Tsinghai, and Shantung, do not yet have comprehensive universities. In Shantung, they have separated the arts and sciences by moving the arts school to Ch'u Fu, "birthplace" of Confucius.

There are a number of universities of national scope, which were the nation's elite institutions of higher learning: Tsinghua University (the Chinese MIT), Peking University, Wuhan University, Nankai University, and Chungshan University. They recruit students from all over the country. These universities, former greats, have extensive libraries, while others have pathetic collections. Such limitations will prevent total equality for many years, but the new admissions policy is intended to bring about greater equality among institutions.

There are six conditions for admission. First, the candidate must be a worker, peasant, or soldier, although since everyone   69 goes to the farm or factory for at least two years after middle school graduation, theoretically everyone is eligible.

The applicant must have graduated from middle school. At the time of our visit there were more junior middle school graduates being admitted than senior middle school graduates because of the cessation of school during the Cultural Revolution. There simply weren't enough recent senior middle school graduates available. The junior middle school graduates require half a year of extra study in math, chemistry, and physics to catch up, but they are helped by advanced students. Eventually some of the best students in the second year classes are junior middle-school graduates. As soon as they have full classes universities will accept only senior middle school graduates.

Chairman Mao has stated that, while the applicant's background counts, his political thought and behavior are most important. The candidate must obtain a recommendation from his coworkers and the approval of the leadership of his work unit.

The remaining three conditions are technical: The candidate should be about 20 years old, in good health (there are no handicapped people at universities), and unmarried (there are few exceptions to this). Academic ability is judged by an interview and middle-school recommendations.

Students have no expenses. They get dormitory rooms, books, and medical care, and money for food and sundries. They are assigned a major on the basis of personal choice tempered by national need.

There are eight classes a day, and two hours a week of militia training. The six-day work week also includes one half day of politics, daily physical education, and one half day of physical labor every two weeks. Like the secondary schools, the universities now have small factories and gardens. Students also give short-term classes at factories. The new experimental college education takes three years, except for theoretical physics, which requires four years because of the extra mathematics. Teachers and students have a monthly self-criticism session.

Every subject that is not a natural science is considered a social science, a science for class struggle. In the factories, natural science theory may be combined with practice. In the arts, society itself is considered the factory. Certain subjects have been completely eliminated (e.g. cultural anthropology), and some people who were trained in one subject are now teaching another.

Teaching methods have been altered to promote more independent thinking. Formerly, university education placed too much emphasis on note-taking. The new system is supposed to encourage stimulation through a process of self-study, whereby students assist one another, and then ask the teacher questions. A current slogan is: "Critical Teaching and Critical Study."

The few classes we saw, however, showed virtually no questioning of the teacher or open discussion, but perhaps this was a tactic to avoid putting one student on the spot before visitors.

Several steps have been taken to equalize the student-teacher relationship. For example, teachers now visit students' dormitories to offer assistance. Examinations no longer screen out students, but rather function as an index of teaching quality. There are no more of what they call "guerilla warfare exams" (sudden attacks). Instead, there are open-book exams, which educate rather than instill fear. Each test is followed by a discussion.

The government has not yet decided how to resolve the problem of graduate studies. It discourages knowledge for its own sake, but also needs quality research. People were not willing to admit to us that only certain individuals could do research. They said that there were no chosen men, only slower and faster learners. Given time, the slow ones can catch up. This is, however, a dilemma that has not been solved.

In the meantime, a new kind of elite does seem to be forming. Undeniably, a college education, since it is still available to only a small percentage of Chinese, creates a special class. The students we met often seemed to come from special institutionally sanctioned revolutionary backgrounds. Perhaps they were chosen to meet us because of this. Nevertheless, the coincidences are interesting. Here are two examples.

Ping Liu-ya worked in the fields for two

years before being accepted as a student in 1970. Her father is a cadre in the PLA, and her mother teaches in a middle school. One sister, 18, is a PLA in a hospital. Her younger brother, 16, and sister, 15, are in middle school, and are both Red Guards. The brother wants to be a PLA after graduation, and the sister hopes to study in the university. Both parents are Party members, and the older sister is a Young Communist League member. The grandparents were peasants in Shantung.

Hung Shao-po had worked in the fields for one year before coming to the university in 1970. Her grandparents were poor employees of a department store in Szechwan, and her father and mother joined the revolution in 1938. Her brother, 22, is an engineer in the Hankow Engineering factory. Two sisters, 25 and 24, work in a semiconductor factory. One sister, 21, is a student in the Wuhan Engineering Institute, and another brother, 17, is a Red Guard in the Wuhan Middle School. Her father is a cadre on the Revolutionary Committee of Hankow, and her mother was a cadre in the Wuhan Library. Both parents are Party members, and all the brothers and sisters are members of the Young Communist League.

There will be future Cultural Revolutions, we are told, because revolution must be a continuing effort. Whether a highly technical and industrial society can be created and maintained in a system of constant revolution and an absence of elites remains to be seen.

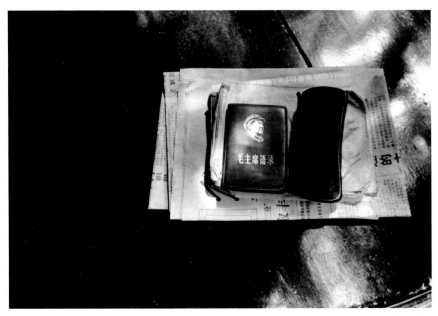

Shanghai

Shanghai

*Shanghai: **T**here are no privately owned cars.*

Canton

The Peking Zoo

The Peking Zoo

Peking

Shanghai: formerly a rich man's estate, now a public park. The men are playing Chinese chess. 75

Although the word commune evokes pastoral images, cities also have communes. A city commune, or worker's village, in Shanghai covers an area of two square kilometers, and is composed of nine villages under the leadership of the Sze Ping Street Revolutionary Committee.

According to the reception committee, a majority of the inhabitants at this commune are workers, with a sprinkling of intelligensia and cadres. Before Liberation this was a wild area containing mostly tombs and other waste areas, as well as thirty to fifty farmers' houses. In 1953, the commune was established for workers who formerly lived in straw huts or on boats.

Currently, the commune has 1,072 apartment buildings, the small ones housing seven to eight families, and the large ones, up to twenty families. We were told that all the apartments have electricity, gas, running water, and flush toilets, and 20 percent have bathtubs. We were then shown what we recognized as a sumptuous apartment consisting of two extremely large rooms, two small rooms, a private kitchen, a private bath with bathtub, and a balcony. It had wooden floors and one unused room— both signs of unusual luxury. This light and

Shanghai

airy apartment rented for twelve yuan a month. The family occupying the apartment was composed of a father who is a cadre for the railway and a graduate of primary school from Anhwei; his wife, also a cadre for the railway and a primary school graduate; their 16-year-old daughter in middle school; a grandfather, a retired railroad worker from Shantung; and a grandmother, who has never been employed. There are four other children who live away from home: a daughter who works on a farm in Anhwei; a son who is a PLA in Fukien; a daughter who is a naval PLA nurse in a hospital in Ningpo; and a son who is married and works in a factory in Sinkiang.

Peking

This is a model new Chinese family. Certainly their assignment to this apartment is an indication of their favored status in the community.

On a return visit to the commune we asked to see a more average home. Three families were living on one floor. Two parents and four children lived in a two-room apartment. Their rent was 5 yuan per month. In another three rooms lived a mother, three sons, and a grandfather. We did not see the third family's rooms. The three families used the same kitchen, located at the head of the stairs. In the kitchen were three separate twin gas burners and three separate food cabinets, one of which was padlocked. All utensils were separate. There was no bathroom in the immediate apartment area, but in a central location, near the kitchen, were two flush toilets which the families on that floor shared.

The city commune also has schools,

shops, a post office, a bank, and a hospital. The Sze Ping commune has seven middle schools with 7,000 students, thirteen primary schools with 12,000 students, and eight kindergartens and nurseries with 1,000 students. Day care for children under four costs 4 yuan per month. Parents pay 3 yuan every six months for children four and above. For older children, the fee is 3 yuan for each six months in primary school and 6 yuan for each six months in middle school. Most factories have free nurseries for newborn babies, but, if the factory is too far away, parents may choose the commune nursery, in which case the factory pays 2 yuan per month of the day-care fee.

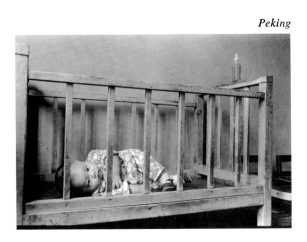

Sze Ping Commune has one central and five branch stores, which sell everything, and include restaurants. They also have commune barbers and tailors, a workers' club, a workers' theater one kilometer away, and a park with animals and pleasure boats 100 feet down the road.

Although most households have at least two workers, husband and wife, many have three or four. Old people or illiterate wives (a legacy from the past) who do not have jobs often run nurseries or do finishing work for other factories. At the Sze Ping Commune we were told that such individuals had organized themselves into eight local factories with 2,000 employees. All the employees are female except for physically defective men, and there are no old men, since they would all either be workers or retired. There is no choice about working in this factory—if you live in this commune, are under forty-five years old, and have no other

work, you must work here. Public opinion would be very harsh toward someone who did not want to work.

Generally the wages in these factories are quite low, 20-30 yuan per month, depending on skill and number of years employment. At one such factory, we saw people making 150,000 flashlight bulbs per day, at another they sew 600–700 suits each day, and at a third, they make silk flowers. The Sze Ping Street Revolutionary Committee not only acts as city manager for the factories, houses, schools, stores, in the commune, but also serves as a court and arbitrator for local disputes, including family problems such as divorce or a parent-child conflict.

Every city area is under the immediate management of a Street Revolutionary Committee. Here again the pyramidal organization allows for efficient management, rapid dissemination of information, and large-scale planning. The Street Revolutionary Committees are managed by the city Revolutionary Committees. They, in turn, are under the jurisdiction of the provincial government, with the exceptions of Shanghai, Tientsin, and Peking, whose Revolutionary Committees function on an equal level with provincial administrations.

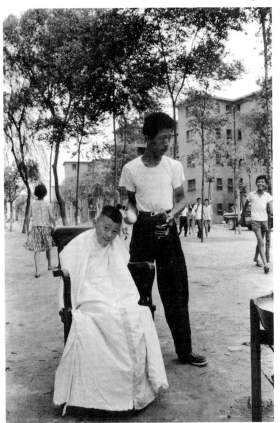

The average Chinese travels long distances by train. The train is usually all hard class, with the exception of one soft-class car in which foreigners and certain Chinese ride. Most of the Chinese we saw in soft class were PLAs and their families.

The trains we rode were clean, comfortable, and punctual. We were somewhat segregated from the other travelers, probably to protect us from staring crowds. When we were not in our private compartment, we were eating in an empty dining car after everyone else was done. Once, feeling very hungry, we went to the dining car on our own, only to be shooed back to our compartment—they had not finished cleaning up.

The meals from Shanghai to Peking consisted of a luncheon for two of chicken and green peppers, sauteed giant shrimps, egg and tomato soup, three sodas, and two bowls of rice—for $1.50. Dinner was pork with bamboo shoots, greens, fish, two bowls of rice, and three orange sodas—for $1.40.

Shanghai

Some travelers carry their own meals or buy local specialties from station vendors. At train stops one may wash utensils in the sinks provided on the platform.

On the Shanghai–Peking train

Station between Shanghai and Peking

COMMUNES

On a train from Urumchi to Shanghai

Yenan: cave dwellings

Sian

Agriculture is the backbone of China's economy—500 million Chinese live and work on farms. It is claimed that the Chinese farmer represents Chairman Mao's contribution to Marxism–Leninism, because it was Chairman Mao who recognized and mobilized the farmer as the Chinese equivalent of the European Marxist worker proletariat.

The Chinese admit that their campaign to make life in the countryside the equal of life in the city still has a long way to go. Farm living standards, particularly in outlying areas, still lag behind those of the city in certain respects, but no one who knew what the country life was like before Liberation has failed to be amazed at the transformation.

View from the Sian–Chengchou train

Yenan

Pataling

Sian

Canton

We visited many different communes, growing a variety of products from rice, corn, and wheat, to vegetables, fruit, and peanuts. Most had pigs, one bred mules, and another, future Peking ducks. The size, terrain, and wealth of these communes varied, but they showed an astonishing uniformity of organization.

Typical of the more prosperous communes is the *Huang-t'u Kung-she* or Yellow Earth Commune, formerly known as the *Sha-t'u Kung-she* or Sand Commune, because of the poor nature of the soil. The commune includes 35,000 people and an area of 69.7 square li (a li is around .5 km.), about 50 percent of which is cultivable. There are fifty-four factories on this commune, which manufacture and repair agricultural machinery, fourteen schools (three middle schools and eleven primary schools), and twelve health stations, of which eleven are clinics and one is a hospital. The commune has 93 tractors, 64 trucks, 600 electric pump wells, and 600 horse carts. The commune is extremely proud of production figures which show continuous increases.

Yenan

The commune was organized in 1958 from four agricultural cooperatives. As a first step after Liberation, mutual aid teams of small groups of farmers were created. Then cooperatives began to form. There were lower ones, considered semi-socialist, in which farmers received rent for the land they contributed, as well as payment for their labor. These later became totally socialist—there was no extra payment for land. Twenty of these upper coops then became one upper-grade large coop, and when Chairman Mao viewed the agricultural situation in Shantung in 1958 and decided that the commune was the answer, four upper-grade large coops became the Yellow Earth Commune.

The major aim of the commune is to unite politics and the commune. To this end the Revolutionary Committee, which manages the Yellow Earth Commune, has five subcommittees dealing with political affairs, production, finance, literature-art-education-and-health, and military matters.

Under the Revolutionary Committee the commune is divided into eleven brigades, which are further divided into 106 production teams. Each production team contains from 45 to over 100 households. The size of the production team is determined by natural area, so each team resembles a village. National need determines the crops these teams grow. Each production unit tries to be self-sufficient in terms of labor, although at busy times they gain the admittedly inefficient assistance of urban students who come to the countryside for their semiannual experience in physical labor (*la lien*).

The government-appointed cadres on the Revolutionary Committee are paid a fixed wage and are supposed to be selected on the recommendation of the masses, with the approval of the leadership. The cadres participate in farm labor one month each year during the commune's busy time. One such cadre, who leads a commune in Shenyang, receives 87 yuan per month and was appointed by the government. These cadres on the Revolutionary Committee, like urban workers, have optional retirement ages and government pensions.

Ordinary farmers are paid on a work-

Canton: making baskets on a commune

point system, based on heaviness of labor. Women never seem capable of earning the highest rating. The value of a work point depends on the total state of the commune at year's end, and thus each person's effort contributes to his fellow members' well-being. For 1971 at the 8–1 Commune outside Shenyang, each farm worker averaged more than 500 yuan, or 5,000+ work points. The top earners had more than 6,000 points, thus earning 600+ yuan, and the lowest made 300 yuan with 3,000 points. Of the commune's income from sales, 63 percent goes for wages, 10 percent for current production, 22 percent for capital expansion, and 5 percent for state agricultural tax.

In addition to wages, farmers have their own houses and small plots of land on which they may raise crops or livestock for private consumption or public sale. In a commune outside Canton these private plots took the form of marked-off areas of an irrigation canal, in which a floating green was being grown to feed private pigs.

Canton: village canal

Shanghai: end of a morning's work

Canton: going home for lunch

91

Peking: the Chinese-Romanian People's Friendship Commune

Peking

Peking

Unlike the urban worker, the farmer gets no maternity leave and no retirement pension or sickness compensation. If he does not work, someone else must support him. Usually other members of his family are available to do so, and since each farm family may have several working members, their combined income may be quite high. Many communes provide an old people's home, called *The Respecting the Old Home,* but most older people prefer to live with their families.

In Sian, Dick met an old farmer whose married sons live with their families in houses next to his, creating a good facsimile of a pre-Liberation extended family. A new aspect of family life has sprung up elsewhere: children who have become PLAs or urban workers.

Most commune members remain at the commune. However, since the Cultural Revolution about thirty members of the Yellow Earth Commune have gone to universities, and none has returned. Some have gone to other communes, and a woman from another commune, who went to an agricultural college, is now in charge of Yellow Earth's fruit trees. Many young people become PLAs for several years, returning later to the commune.

Farm people marry slightly earlier than city people—21 for women and 25 for men. It would be unheard of for people over 30 never to have been married. Divorce is rare —of 4,400 households on the 8–1 commune, there only have been an estimated 3 to 5 divorces, all based on incompatibility, in the last five years.

Not every commune is well off. Certain undeveloped places are designated as hardship areas, to which young people who have graduated from middle school volunteer to go to develop the land. During the many years when the potential commune has no income, volunteers are paid a small sum, around 17 yuan per month, out of which they must buy all their food. These young volunteers may become labor heroes like the residents of Tachai, China's most famous production brigade, if and when the commune fluorishes — many years hence.

Peking: a family album

Yenan: a worker's hero holding a photograph of himself and Chairman Mao

Sian: a farmer's home

The communes we visited were all prosperous, and the farmers' houses were without exception roomy and well furnished. They all had electricity, and each home had electric lights. In many cases, the houses were less crowded than those in the city and contained several rooms, a private kitchen, and a little garden patch. Many of the farmers had what are commonly called the three rounds and one sound: a watch, a bicycle, a sewing machine, and a radio.

Yenan

Several of the hospitals we visited were famous before Liberation, and others were opened later. The Tientsin hospital was opened in 1966. The Shenyang Medical College started as a Red Army Health School Hospital in Kiangsi, participated in the Long March, and operated in Yenan for eight years before moving to the northeast. It is located in a former Kuomintang hospital, which before that was a Japanese medical college. Our tour included the underground bunker where the Japanese performed secret bacteriological experiments, and a display of scholarly articles, written by the Japanese doctors in several languages, detailing the results of experiments they had performed on "healthy Chinese brains."

Chairman Mao's medical line is that science must be oriented toward the service of the workers, peasants, and soldiers. Just what that means has been the subject of much discussion and thought. Currently, medical education, like university education, is in a state of reorganization. Medical training which used to take six years now takes three years of study, and an indefinite period of residency in a hospital. Medical students were being recruited both from ninth-grade and twelfth-grade graduates from before the Cultural Revolution. The ninth-grade graduates receive an extra half year of training in biology and chemistry. Every student has served at least two years as a worker, peasant, or soldier. Training has been cut down to suit the student's specialty. A student who is not going to be an orthopedist need not memorize all the bones in the human body. Choice of specialty is governed by students' interests modified by the needs of the country.

Occasionally, a barefoot doctor, after practicing for a few years, is chosen to continue his medical education, but in general he remains rooted in the country. After six months training as a paraprofessional, he participates half time in the production process and does medical practice half time.

Throughout the educational process, both student and teacher continue to work in rural areas. The Shenyang Medical College is connected with a commune 200 miles away where each student spends three weeks every semester. In addition, the doctors and other workers on the hospital staff rotate, in three-month shifts, as medical staff on this commune. With this system, each staff member only goes to the farm once in several years, yet the farm has continuous good medical care.

We were told that mental illness has been greatly reduced because there is no more venereal disease (the Canton Hospital cannot find a case for teaching purposes), no great competition, no love triangles, no hunger and cold, no occupational problems, and democratic family life. I took some of these statements with a grain of salt.

There is no more electroshock therapy. The basic therapeutic method is the *t'an-hsin* (heart-to-heart talk). These talks, either on a one-to-one basis or one to a group, involve showing the patient that his problems are not so great, and that he should look beyond himself to how he can help China achieve her goals. The doctors say that social stimuli are most important, and that tranquilizers such as chloropromazine are used only to enable the patient to talk with the therapist.

The Chinese reported some small success in using acupuncture to treat the symptoms of schizophrenia. While the overt behavior is controlled, the patient may continue to suffer delusions and other emotional disorders. This technique has been used for five years in Canton. The average hospital stay for schizophrenics was reported as three to six months.

Our requests to visit mental hospitals and talk with staff members were all refused. As far as we could tell, all the mental hospitals were in the countryside. We did learn that, of the 1,000 patients in the municipal mental hospital for Kwangtung Province, most are schizophrenics. One Shenyang doctor reported that his attempts to use acupuncture and training in the treatment of 300 mentally retarded patients were unsuccessful.

There are occasional suicides. A Canton doctor's view was that suicide attempts could be attributed to conflict among the

Sian: commune hospital

people, or expression by one person against the group. When one individual operates against the group, the therapeutic emphasis is on reform, on how to be a man. The importance of interpersonal relations is stressed. To treat a suicidal patient, doctors first consider his type of employment, personal relationships, and how he perceives the meaning of life. Then they may attempt to instill in him a sense of revolutionary optimism, getting him to think of the larger picture.

There is no sex education in the schools, but birth-control information and devices are widely available. My cousins tell me that girls still don't talk to each other about sex, and neither do boys. Instead, they figure it out from biology, which they study at around 15 or 16. However, when they were 11 or 12, a female teacher took my female cousins aside and told them about menstruation. Sex manuals are available in the bookstores.

Abortion is available on demand, but husbands must agree. The wife's local organization (the manager of her factory or work unit) must also agree; if both husband and wife want the abortion, then the work authorization may not be necessary. A family with two or three children is considered ideal. A couple with no children who want an abortion are considered odd, but they may get permission. For a pregnancy under three months, the suction method is used. I was told that the process takes half a day. In fact, while I was being examined in the Wuhan Hospital a woman on a table next to mine was having an abortion by suction. She seemed unanesthetized and walked away unassisted. She was followed by another patient. The entire process seemed to take no more than five to ten minutes. (If I had not been Chinese, I suspect I would have been examined in a private room.)

After the abortion, the wife receives a paid, two-week rest period at home. While there are a few reports of unwed mothers, their situation is viewed as a matter of reeducation of the parties involved.

Trained midwives generally assist at childbirth. They have more training than the barefoot doctors, and are able to insert

Peking

intrauterine devices. Many village women deliver their children at home, although all are free to go to the local midwife hospital.

The hospitals we visited varied only slightly in general organization. Each medical staff consists of a chief of each department, visiting doctors, and residents who remain in that position for an indefinite period, until their skills are considered satisfactory.

The employees at Tientsin Orthopedic Hospital were ranked on a salary scale from 1 to 26, with 1 being the highest at 320 yuan per month, and 26 the lowest at 32 yuan—for new graduates. Doctors start at 46 yuan and are promoted in a year to 56. Most doctors cluster around rank 10, 110 yuan. There is another cluster, from ranks 12 to 16, of nurses, technicians, and doctors with only high school educations.

Nurses' salaries in Peking range from 40–130 yuan, and administrators' salaries from 40–140 yuan. Doctors' salaries in Peking range from 50–330 yuan. When I asked if all the highest paid doctors were from pre-Liberation days, I was answered with a sensitive no. Some of these doctors' high salaries were cut back during the Cultural Revolution, but they have been restored, with interest. It was explained that it is hard for people who have been accustomed to a certain standard to adjust to a lower one. New doctors earn lower salaries, and eventually doctors' salaries will come down to the same general range as that of nurses and administrators. This same system of allowing professionals from pre-Liberation days to continue to earn high salaries also applies to university professors.

Effort is made to prevent the formation of doctor-elites by requiring periodic trips to the country and attendance at study sessions. In Peking, the doctors spend five to six hours a week in study sessions. Doctors and nurses study separately from the cadres.

Although there is a retirement age, the Ji Hsueh Tan Hospital in Peking claims that they have never had a single doctor retire.

The Peking hospital, with a staff of over 800, is administered by a sixteen-member Revolutionary Committee, including three nurses, two doctors, six PLAs, and six cadres. Five members are women. Over half the doctors in this hospital are women.

The hospital-clinic we visited in Shanghai is on the lowest of the three tiers of city-wide organization. There are sixteen such hospitals in the district. It serves only people from the immediate area. The next tier includes three hospitals and four or five sanitoriums. At the top is the biggest hospital in the city. The nature of the illness determines the hospital to which the patient is sent. The hospital we visited has no beds but includes dental facilities. For inpatient care, a patient would go to one of the three nearby hospitals in the second tier.

We were told that social service departments are unnecessary now that every patient has his own unit (work, school, etc.) to take care of him and his family. In case of illness or injury, the worker continues to receive his salary. All workers in schools and work units other than factories (stores, restaurants, etc.) have their fees paid monthly by the state, much like a charge account, at public expense. Dependents are the individual's responsibility, but a medical allowance is given by the work unit. No one's living standard need be lowered because of illness. Factory workers have their medical fees paid by the factory under the labor welfare system. In addition, one-half of the worker's parents' and childrens' fees will be paid by the factory. The civil affairs department of the city government pays the fees of anyone who does not fit into these categories. The Revolutionary Street Committee of the individual's neighborhood helps him arrange payment. All medical fees are very low.

Children who have to stay in the hospital for a long time get schooling there. The hos-

Yenan: fly-extermination poster

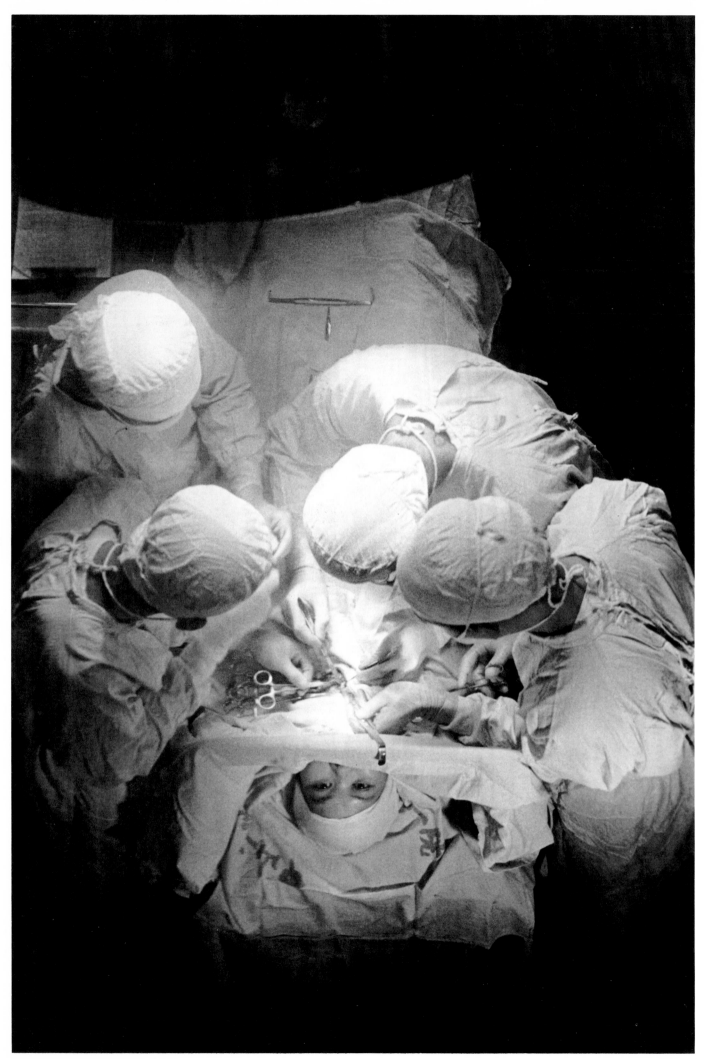

Canton: thyroid surgery with acupuncture anesthesia

pital corresponds with the schools to get each child's record, and the class program is structured to the individual child's needs.

I witnessed six surgical procedures using acupuncture anesthesia. Only in one knee operation did the patient seem at all uncomfortable. The other patients were completely at ease. One patient undergoing open-brain surgery, although a bit groggy, was able to speak with the nurse, welcome us, and eat a couple of orange slices from a jar.

Most medical research in China today is concerned with acupuncture, an ancient Chinese science which became the subject of serious study only after the Cultural Revolution. Its function is not yet understood, and its application to new areas, such as mental illness, is being examined.

The increased use of acupuncture is part of the attempt to combine Western and Chinese medicine. For example, the treatment of bone fractures, which we observed in the orthopedic hospital in Tientsin, does not, as in the West, require an operation or a hard cast. Instead, the area of fracture is covered with Chinese medical plaster, and soft padding and a small splint are placed at the point where the damaged bone must move

back into position. The patient then follows a regular program of exercises, including some *Tai Chi Chuan* movements, which increase in difficulty as the bone heals.

We saw no evidence to contradict the Chinese claim that most infectious diseases have been eliminated through inoculation and sanitation control. One doctor said that their most serious current problems are cardiovascular disease and cancer.

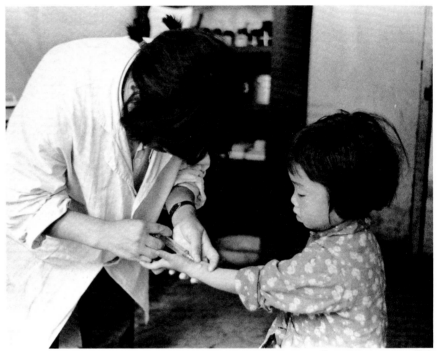

Canton: commune clinic

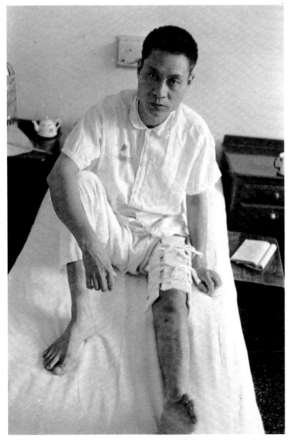

Canton: commune clinic

Adequate medical care for all is an important goal of the Chinese government. The cost is minimal (in Yenan the fee is 1.50 yuan per year, and in Shenyang 1 yuan per year), with the brigade paying any remaining balance. Medical service at the many clinics and hospitals in each commune is adequate for the usual needs, although exceptionally complicated cases may be sent to city hospitals. The staffs at the clinics are comprised mainly of barefoot doctors.

In Shanghai we saw some ingenious inventions designed for rural areas: a small portable x-ray unit, weighing only 25 pounds, that can be folded into its own suitcase and takes x-rays in bright sunlight; a 15-pound portable examining table with stirrups and a portable light that can be operated in the absence of electricity by pedaling a stationary bicycle unit.

101

Shanghai: commune

To make the countryside more appealing and more self-sufficient, the government has tried to bring such amenities as stores, plays, movies, and television to the farms. The same Shanghai exhibit showed a portable movie screen and projector, which, like the examining table light, could be operated in the absence of electricity by a bicycle-powered unit. Entertainers from the big cities fulfill their physical labor quota by performing in rural areas.

In pre-Liberation times, as old farmers will tell you, rural life for the poor farmer was miserable. Descriptions of the wealth and oppression of the landlords were generally accurate. Starvation and misery were rampant. We saw no evidence of hunger or sickness. All the children we saw were attending schools near their homes. Some families even seemed prosperous; they all seemed adequately fed, housed, and clothed, and they all knew why. Every farm home we visited featured, in a place of honor, a portrait of Chairman Mao. There can be no doubt that the Chinese farmer has found a dedicated guardian.

Shanghai: commune store

Canton: commune factory

Every commune includes small factories to produce and repair equipment needed on the commune. Some of the factories are quite rudimentary, but one, for example, produces hundreds of mechanical threshers for many of the communes in the province. By putting factories out in the countryside, and by developing major industries in every province, the government is continuing a drive toward decentralization and self-sufficiency which it began in the caves of Yenan.

Shanghai

Sian

Yenan

Yenan

109

Canton

Canton